How It Happened

by Gary Clarke

How It Happened
© 2016. Gary Clarke. All rights reserved.

Published in the USA by:
BearManor Media
P O Box 71426
Albany, Georgia 31708
www.bearmanormedia.com

Printed in the United States of America
ISBN   978-1-59393-946-5 (paperback)

Book design by Darlene Swanson • www.van-garde.com
Cover and Back designed by Ava L'Amoreaux

Contents

Preface

This book can be construed one of two ways, and for those more aggressively inclined, two of two ways, and those are these:

A coffee table reader where visiting friends and family remark,

"I've heard marvelous things about this book. May I?" And you respond,

"Of course. And, ah . . . watch your coffee cup."

The second is the ever present, always welcome "John Reader." Multi-taskers find this type of a book most rewarding simply because the laughter that the reading creates facilitates the "other" task.

My journey through the entertainment industry, which began in high school, has put me in touch with some of the most extraordinary people on the planet. "People" people. If you're reading this, you're one of them. I'm talking about actors, singers, dancers, comics, story-tellers, street performers, AND the people who watch them/us. You!

Laughter and spreading it is truly a passion for me, and telling stories about things that have passed my way, exaggerated or not, has been a great way to do that.

This book is literally "How It Happened." Not from the point-of-view of a world-renowned movie icon but from a guy who did okay working in the profession he loves. A guy who has been awestruck by movies and movie stars from the time he first said, "Can we see the cartoon again, mommy?"

I've sat at my computer, reminiscing romantically about the days, months and years of my life, and find myself laughing a lot. I've shed a few tears as well. Then again, there's no funny without a little serious.

This book is a way for me to say thank you for the wonders you've brought into my life as I was trying to bring the same to you.

Gary Clarke

What's In A Name?

For the sake of clarity, it should be mentioned here that I have two names: Gary Clarke, my "professional" name, and Clarke L'Amoreaux, my surname. We will bounce back and forth between the two until the explanation of the "birth" of the name "Gary Clarke." From that point on, to avoid any confusion, we'll use Gary.

Obligatory Baby Pictures

| 18 mo | 8 yrs First Communion | 10 yrs |

ONE – The Seed Is Planted

Everyone does the Senior Play in high school. Well, most everyone. I did. I was seventeen. Woodrow Wilson High, in the East Los Angeles town of El Sereno, was presenting *Quiet Summer* (1951) as performed by the senior class of 1951, and it would be staged in the gym, as were most school events. I played the hero, the lead, you know, the one with the most lines. Diane French was the female lead. That's important because her mom's date for opening night was Doc Bishop, a well-known talent scout from 20th Century Fox. He was the guy who discovered Shirley Temple, among others. After the show, he approached me and introduced himself. *Sure*, I thought. *A 20th Century Fox talent scout scouting an east L.A. high school senior play? I don't think so.* But Diane and her mom confirmed it . . . him . . . the talent scout part. He was very complimentary. He said he'd kept track of how many times I stole a scene. A bunch. Then he said that he'd like me to come out to the studio and meet "a few people." I told him it would take me at least fifteen minutes to get ready, but he assured me that the following week would be just fine. Reluctantly, I agreed to wait.

Then came the day. 20th Century Fox Studio is located in that part of L.A. that is today known as Century City. In fact, Century City used to be the back lot of that famous studio. There was a pass waiting for me at the gate. I marveled my way through parts of the lot and was riveted by the buildings and streets and sets that I'd

A camera! Oh, boy!

seen in so many movies. A scaled-down version of an "el" (elevated train) right out of the Bronx was impressive. I saw Tyrone Power walking by with two beautiful women. I couldn't tell who the women were because I tripped over a sprinkler.

The meeting with Mr. Bishop (he said I could call him Doc) went very well. He introduced me to directors, producers, talent coordinators, and bought me lunch in the commissary. He spoke frankly. He wanted to put me under contract. Build me and make me a 20th Century Fox star. Be a part of "The Team." Give me a dressing room and everything! Just one problem. I was only seventeen. Not yet legal.

"We want to wait till you're eighteen," he said. "That's just a few months away and I don't want to go through the rigmarole of dealing with parents. I've already got a few pictures in mind. So, as soon as you turn eighteen, call me. Meanwhile, don't get arrested, don't join the army, don't leave the country, don't get married. Understood?" I said I understood and asked if I could see my dressing room. He said no.

I didn't join the army, I didn't leave the country, I didn't get arrested. I got married. Marilyn, my high school sweetheart. Why? Don't ask me. I was seventeen going on twelve. What did I know? But I had been around some! Catalina Island and Tijuana—a couple of times. Married in October. Called Doc in November.

Rinnnnggg

Doc: Doc Bishop, here.

Clarke: Hi Doc. Clarke L'Amoreaux. Wilson High School. How are you?

Doc: Fine, Clarke. And you?

Clarke: Great. Well, I turned eighteen.

Doc: I know. August, wasn't it?

Do I look like
a "Clarke" to you?

Clarke: Yes. The sixteenth.

Doc: It's November.

Clarke: Yeah. Already. I've been working and stuff.

Doc: I understand you got married.

Clarke: I . . . uh . . . well . . . yeah, I . . . did. . . .

Click. Bzzzzzzzzzzz. . . .

Clarke: Hello. Doc? Hello. . . .

Love was the cause of it all.
(That's Marilyn on the right)

I called back, and Doc's secretary told me that he wasn't in, nor would he be should I ever call again. "People only disappoint Doc once and you've had your once," she said.

And that was that. It was all over. I was out before I was in. However, if I was honest—which I am—I'd admit that down deep I just knew that Doc would have second thoughts and call me back. He'd beg my forgiveness for hanging up on me and plead with me to forget our differences and join his 20th Century Fox family. Would I forgive? Would I forget? Are you kidding? You bet your noogies I would. But, alas, there were no calls, from Doc or anyone else.

My lot was cast. I worked as an assistant dealer for the L.A. Examiner delivering, door-to-door, nine hundred papers a day and thirteen hundred on Sundays. Did that for the next four years, during which time I also had three children—all boys. Jeff, Dennis and David. Dennis and David were born in the same year, Dennis in February, and David in December. I probably shouldn't have snuck into the hospital that night after Dennis was born. It wasn't till after David was born that anyone told me where babies came from. I was such a dweeb!

I could always go back to my old job.

It was a tumultuous marriage and it ended nastily after four years.

I was on my own and the future looked bleak. "Bleak" as perceived by any twenty-two year-old going on fourteen. Oh, yes. I had grown during my marriage.

TWO – Out of the Ashes

When the bug bites, it bites deep, and the acting bug that bit me had very long teeth.

Once bitten, there's no cure. The germ lies dormant, waiting for the opportune moment to infiltrate the "acting" atoms of your DNA's double helix. There's no warning, no telltale signs, no blurring of vision. It just hits you. One night, you'll never know when, you'll wake from a sound sleep, sit bolt upright in bed and scream, "I'VE GOT TO ACT!"

Then, having no idea from whence it came, you rattle off a stream of words Shakespearian:

My brother, Pete, Pop and "Clarke," actors all.

"Yea, verily I say unto thee, thee who hast said naught but vile inflammatories projected violently upon my person which hath heretofore worn only the torn breeches from which my butt protrudeth." Don't bother looking it up. You won't find it anywhere but here.

Pasadena Comeuppance

When I could stand it no longer, I called my high school drama teacher, Miss Aura Hoffman—Oh, how I loved that woman—and asked if she might get me an audition at the prestigious Pasadena Playhouse. She said she'd try. Now this part is important as an explanation of continuity, so pay attention. At this point in time I was in my delivering-900-papers-a-day mode. I started work at 1 a.m., which meant I went to bed about 7 p.m., which I had done on this particular night. The phone rang at 8 p.m. In my sleep stupor I answered.

Clarke: Hullo.

A thick Russian accent spoke back to me.

Madame: May I spick with Mr. Clarrrke L'Amorrreaux, plis.

Clarke: Spicking.

Madame: I am Madam Roboskaya, Artistic Director for Pasadena Playhouse. I have spoken with my dear friend, Aura Hoffman, who tells me that you would be valuable asset to our playhouse.

Clarke: Uh, huh.

Madame: Ve are doing ze play *Bernardine*, and would like you to audition for part. Tomorrow, 6:30, third floor, back of Playhouse, room 8. Can you be there?

Clarke: Uhh . . . okay . . . yeah.

Madame: You will meet director, Chuck Brandywine, who will conduct audition. Goot luck.

Clarke: Yeah . . . okay . . . see ya.

Can I impress 'em or what?

Beautiful building, the Playhouse. Always reminded me of an early California mission. Stately. Commanding respect. It was dark when I arrived. 7:30. I know. She said 6:30, but I didn't want to appear too anxious. Besides, I was good. I played all the leads at Wilson high. Terrific reviews in our school paper. I would probably put the Pasadena Playhouse back on the map. Confidently I mounted the stairs that led to a covered walkway attached to the side of the building, overlooking Colorado Boulevard. At the very end I turned left into a short, narrow hallway illuminated only by a single light bulb dangling precariously from a frayed cord that disappeared abruptly into the dark ceiling above.

I found room 8, opened the door, and blurted out, "Hi. This where you're auditioning for Bernardine?" It was only then that I noticed about fifteen people seated quietly about the small room.

Someone dropped a pin. It shattered my eardrums. A very serious, important-looking gentleman fixed me with a withering look and intoned icily, "Yes. And you've just interrupted a reading. Please, take a seat."

I discovered quickly that this was the director, Chuck Brandywine. I don't know how I got to a chair but I did, trying to look as much like the wallpaper as possible. I sat and I watched and I listened. Something was wrong. In all the auditions I'd done (seven), and all the plays I'd been in (five), I'd never seen or heard the kind of acting I was watching there. At least not at Wilson High. These people were good. I mean good.

It was an eternity before they got to me. An eternity of trepidation, doubt and sweating. Perhaps they'd run out of audition time. Given the shape I was in, that possibility sounded great. No such luck.

"Clarke. Would you please read the part of 'Beau.' Top of page 13."

I stood, made my way to the front of the room, and opened my script. I opened it but could not see it. This was not the way auditions went in Miss Hoffman's class.

NOTE: Scripts have dialogue and they have stage directions. You audition by reading the dialogue, not the stage directions.

Clarke: "Ahh . . . Beau enters . . . ah . . . Stage Right . . . Hi, Mr. Welder, I mean, Weldy. Hi, Mr. Weldy. I'll bet I'm surprised . . . you're surprised I'm here."

Chuck saved my butt. "Clarke," he said. "It's alright. Everybody gets nervous at these things. I'll tell you what. . . ." He turned to his assistant. "Jeremy, take Clarke into the next room and run the lines with him. Go with Jeremy, Clarke. Relax, go over the scene and come back when you're ready. Okay?"

I agreed and followed Jeremy into the room across the hall. We read over the scene a few times and I relaxed. Jeremy was polite, professional, and an all-around huge help. He asked if I was ready and I said I was. "Just give me a minute to compose myself and I'll come right in." He agreed and left.

I'd always been a quick study, and this scene was only two pages. Piece o' cake. Six or eight minutes later the lines were memorized. Tunnel vision gone. I was ready! I was going to knock their socks off. I exited my room and re-made my entrance into the audition room.

It was dark. Quiet. Empty. Not a soul to be seen anywhere. They'd left me. The bastards took off with nary a word. I was pissed. I was embarrassed. I was alone on the third floor of the Pasadena Playhouse with that damned dangly light bulb. Definitely a life-altering moment. A learning moment. I vowed to never allow something like that to happen to me again. So much for vows. It did happen again. In spades. But not right away.

THREE – Back To The Old Drawing Board

I guess I was just too dumb to quit. I figured there must be something salvageable out of all those years (two) in drama class. So . . . I started haunting any and all of the Little Theater groups in and around L.A.

Over the next few years I must have been in over sixty plays, performing in every venue imaginable—proscenium, theater-in-the-round, high school auditoriums, gymnasiums, converted houses, public parks and/or swimming pools, truck beds, rodeo arenas, old barns—you get the picture. By the way, if you were to ask me what I'd change if given the opportunity, I'd say, "Not a damn thing!" Invaluable experiences.

Like the open-sided barn in St. George, Utah, for example. Six of us who had been performing at the Glendale Center Theater in Glendale, CA, drove to St. George to perform under a few of the unique circumstances just mentioned. Ruth and Nathan Hale, Mormon owners of the GCT, had arranged it and managed to get us all a small stipend and gas money as well. We didn't care. It was an adventure; we were doing what we loved and we liked each other.

After opening night (we were there a week), we had to alter the script a bit to include the vast array of insects, bats, and other flying things we'd never seen before. These adorable tiny creatures,

Arsenic and Old Lace at Glendale Center Theater.
That's me with the night stick.

attracted by the stage lights, would fly in and out of the sideless barn, into the scenes, into our mouths and hair, and build nests. Needless to say, they were hard to ignore.

On the second night, however, we were prepared. Every member of the cast carried either a butterfly net, a fly-swatter, or a Flit spray can. We were ruthless *and* we didn't miss a cue or a line. We even added a line or two to justify what we were doing:

Bat flies into the scene and tries to fly off with leading lady's hair.

Leading man catches said bat in butterfly net, holds it up and announces brightly: "Doris, I think this would make an exquisite hat."

The audience loved it and wanted us to stay over another week. We declined, graciously.

I did fifteen or twenty shows at GCT, and during that time,

several agents would show up to check out the local talent. One guy, short, cherubic, in his mid-thirties, was very taken with me and assured me that he could make me a star (shades of Doc Bishop!). He talked a good story and even introduced me to a couple of casting directors—at least he *said* they were casting directors. Maybe they were. What did I know? Eventually, as in life, the truth will out, which was that he wasn't interested in making me a star; he wanted to marry me and have my baby. I declined, graciously, and broke his heart. I have often wondered if maybe . . . Naw, probably wouldn't have worked. He was a Democrat.

Enter Byron

Another agent who showed up was a gentleman by the name of Byron Griffith. A real agent. Not a big, famous one, but legit. He spoke with a deep, affected, Shakespearian voice developed over years of practice. And tall. About 6' 3." You could say that he was a bit over the top and liked it that way. Don't know where he got his money, but he was well off. He owned a large, fifty-year-old, three-story house on the corner of Hollywood Boulevard and

Byron: "Yes, but can he act?"

Laurel Canyon. The first floor was huge and decorated in a cross between art-deco, gothic, and early Pier One, and it was that part of the house in which he dwelt. We called it Merlin's Cave. It also had four apartments that he rented out. Three were occupied. The other was available at $50 a month. Steep at the time, but I took it.

The tenants: 1) An actor, struggling, early twenties. Nice looking. Quiet. I forgot his name; 2) A nice young lady. Secretary. Mid-twenties, kind of heavy-set and loved to drive fast. I forgot her name, too; 3) An aspiring, eighteen-year-old actress whose name I do remember: Connie Stevens. If you don't remember her, look her up on IMDB. A blonde-haired, blue-eyed Italian, feisty, cute as a button, and a soon-to-be very important factor in my life.

FOUR – A Guy Has to Eat!

During all of the aforementioned, I held down many jobs, e.g., installing chain link fences, stock boy in a grocery store, mason (building block walls), construction, hauled hay, delivery boy, yard maintenance, machinist, and more. When Byron found me, I was making good money working in a machine shop in San Gabriel, California, eight or ten miles east of El Sereno. And the hours—7 a.m. to 3:30 p.m.—didn't interfere with my burgeoning career. I'd work during the day and audition, rehearse, or perform at night. By the way, with the exception of our stint in St. George, I did not get paid for Little Theater/Community Theater work.

From Grimley to Grease Paint

There were five machinists in this shop, which was run by a short, chunky, no-nonsense Englishman. Mr. Grimley. Good boss, but completely devoid of humor. Not mean, just humorless. Be on time, get your work done, do it well, and your check was never late. I was sure I had seen him in the movie *A Christmas Carol* as one of the street vendors. He vehemently denied it. He was also quite gullible, which left him wide open for virtually any joke concocted by me or my colleagues. *Really? Like what?* I'll tell you.

The clock in the shop clicked from minute to minute—no second hand. Perfect for our little caper. The five of us had it all planned. Grimley was always at his desk when we arrived at 7 a.m., and he would stay there doing whatever good bosses do to keep their business going. While we would usually bid him a good morning, on this particular morning, which happened to be *April 1st*, we didn't say anything. In fact, we looked sullen, pissed off, perturbed, disgruntled, and not at all happy. Grimley's reaction was minimal. From 7 to 7:30, no one said a word. We got a couple of quizzical looks from him, but he got nothing from us.

If you had been there, this is what you would have seen: The clock clicks to 7:30, Dean shuts of his lathe, mutters an audible "Shit!" and heads for the bathroom. Grimley tries to say something but is ignored. 7:32, Jerry shuts off his lathe and pours himself a cup of coffee. Grimley's brow is now furrowed. 7:34, Royal and Neil shut off their lathes, huddle in conference, and glance occasionally in Grimley's direction. By now Dean is back at his lathe, glowering. 7:35, I shut off my lathe and proceed to loudly throw tools into my toolbox. The others do the same and, with nary a word, we stomp out of the shop. I manage a look back and see Grimley standing at his desk, his jaw resting on a stack of invoices. We slam the door

Not Grimley's, but sort of.

behind us and move quickly to the back door, which we had previously unlocked. We wait about two minutes, yank open the door, burst in, and shout, "APRIL FOOL!"

Grimley was frozen, or perhaps catatonic would be the more appropriate term. We thought for a moment he had died standing up. Then, what did we know about Englishmen? Then his eyes blinked, the side of his mouth turned upward, a smile (a first for us), and then he erupted into the loudest, most raucous laughter you can imagine. We'd never, ever seen this side of Grimley. He kept laughing for ten minutes while the five of us got back to work. And every so often, throughout the rest of the day, he would burst into paroxysms of laughter. It was a good day all around.

Then there was another day, seemingly just an ordinary day at Grimley's Machine Shop, when I received a phone call. Grudgingly, Grimley told me to take it in his office. I did. It was Byron, my agent.

"Clarke," he intoned. I thought for a moment it was Vincent Price. "They are casting for a teenage motorcycle movie, and I believe I can get you a part as a member of the good gang, and they want to see you in two hours. Shall I tell them you'll be here?"

"Well . . . ah . . . I'm working, Byron, and Mr. Grimley doesn't like. . . ."

"Fine," said an annoyed Byron. "I'll tell them you're too busy to make it." "Wait!" I said, realizing that the door to stardom had opened and I was reluctant to enter. A long pause, then: "I'll be there."

My mind was spinning. What if I didn't get the job? And what if Grimley fired me for leaving work? Take an early lunch? No. Not enough time. Take a late lunch? No. Same problem. Wait! I had it!

About ten minutes after "the call," I ran to the bathroom, locked the door and proceeded to make the most disgusting and loud puking sounds I could muster. I was sure everyone heard. I came out of the bathroom and told Grimley that I was dying and asked if I could go because I would rather die at home than draped over a lathe. He

understood, and I was out the door.

One hour and forty-five minutes later found me at the office of the producer who was casting the movie *Dragstrip Riot (1957)*. The office was full of actors, as was the hallway. I found a spot at the end of the line. I was only there for a minute when Byron appeared out of nowhere, grabbed my arm, and ushered me past the crowd and into the producer's office. He introduced me.

"Clarke, this is Dale Ireland, the producer. Mr. Ireland, Clarke L'Amoreaux." We shook hands. He looked at Byron, pointed to me, and said, "We'll have to do something about that name." He motioned for me to sit. I did. For about thirty seconds. Things were said—I knew not what—and I was then ushered back out into the hall.

"That's it?" I said, dumbfounded. "That was my interview? That's why I left work and jeopardized my job? What the hell just happened??" Byron smiled haughtily. "You're a member of the good gang. Congratulations." And he was gone.

It took a while for everything to sink in, so I remember very little about driving back to San Gabriel except that by the time I got home I had realized that I was going to be in a movie. I'd forgotten to ask Byron how much I was to be paid, but it seemed irrelevant compared to the fact that I WAS GOING TO BE IN A MOVIE!! I took the rest of day off and called everyone in the East L.A. phonebook to tell them of my good fortune.

However, I couldn't tell the guys at work for fear that Grimley would find out. I had to keep mum. The next morning, Grimley asked how I was feeling. I must have had a "Huh?" expression on my face because he pressed the matter.

"Are you still throwing up?"

"Oh, that," I said, bouncing back to reality. "I'm fine. Completely cured."

"Good," he said handing me my day's work order. "Get to work."

Everyone, I mean everyone, was fighting
for a part in the much touted *Dragstrip Riot.*

I did, and I was on Cloud Nine. I was in a movie! A member of the "good gang." I wondered if that was better than being a member of the "bad gang." I didn't care. I'd gotten the part. The day was going swimmingly—until lunch. The five of us were eating outside, telling jokes and insulting one another, when Grimley interrupted us.

"Clarke. A phone call. My office. And let's not make this a habit."

"Clarke? Byron. It seems they've lost the male lead for *Dragstrip Riot,* and Mr. Ireland is looking desperately for a replacement. He must find him this week. He's auditioning now and you might have a chance if you can get down here quickly. What shall I tell him?"

I had a "relapse," and Grimley sent me home before I could puke on his shoes or die in his shop. I made it back to the auditions in less than an hour. Every unknown and not-very-well-known actor was there, including a few guys who'd never acted in their lives. It was a full-blown cattle call. Old guys trying to look young; young kids trying to look older. A three-ring circus with hundreds of clowns trying to make it to the center ring, and I was right in the middle of it all. Let it be noted here that that day was the last day I worked at Grimley's.

This audition wasn't your run-of-the-mill audition. First I'd read for the director, then I'd read for the producer, then they'd ask me to wait and read again. This went on for five days, during which time I watched acting hopefuls come and go. Then there were those who had been there every day, a few of whom had already been cast. Connie was one of them. She, too, was a member of the good gang and never stopped talking about what a terrific actor I was. She was particularly vociferous when the director and producer were around. It was hard not to pay attention to Connie. Tony Butala was cast as well and would serve as the "musical relief" for the film. Steve Ihnat was cast as one of the bad guys. Out of hundreds of guys, there were just two of us who were still in contention for the part of "Rick," the lead in *Dragstrip Riot*. I racked my brain for something, anything I might do to "get that part."

Around the third or fourth day, Byron told me that the powers that be thought the lead should be a blonde. Great! My hair was brown. "I'm not saying it would sway them, hinted Byron. "But, if you were to show up as a blonde, well. . . . "

Blondes *Do* Have More Fun

My mother was an office manager for a Magic Mirror beauty salon. She'd been following this saga and had all her friends convinced that I was soon to be the next Tyrone Power (who had black hair) and/or Clark Gable (who also had black hair). So Liz, one of the beauticians who agreed with my mom about which star I would replace, agreed to bleach my hair—for nothing. It didn't make sense! All the movie heroes I knew had <u>black</u> hair: John Wayne, Gable and Power, Henry Fonda, Gary Cooper, go through the list. Okay,

Two blondes.
Yvonne's the short one.

there was Van Johnson, but still. . . . At 3 a.m., the morning after the day Byron had said, "But, if you were to turn up as a blonde . . ." there I was, sitting in Liz's kitchen, draped in a cape, dripping bleach, scalp burning, waiting to turn blonde. I'm just glad that Liz was friendly. Very friendly.

By now most everyone who'd been cast, good gang *and* bad gang, had become friends and seemed to be pulling for me, so I wasn't surprised when they erupted in cheers as I walked into the office later that morning looking blonder than Jayne Mansfield. Dale, the producer, and David, the director, came out of their office to investigate the commotion. They looked at me several times before recognition clicked in. They just stood there, dumbfounded. Connie piped up: "Well. You said the lead should be blonde." More cheers from the "gang." Two days later I got the part. Not because I was the best actor (I wasn't), and not because I gave the best reading (I didn't), but because I wanted the part bad enough to do just about anything to get it, and the producer recognized that. Oh, and Magic Mirror closed the shop for a day of celebration. I think Liz got a raise.

Connie

I first met Connie in Byron's living room. He had asked me to bring a scene from a play I'd done at GCT—a comedy. Connie and I were to learn the scene and audition for the casting people at Universal Studios, a big deal at that time. We started rehearsing, and Connie was playing her part like Camille. I explained that the play we were reading was a comedy and not some heavy, dark drama. She argued that it was a drama. Occasionally, I re-asserted that it was a comedy, but nope, she stood her ground. Man, talk about stubborn. At one point, when she stopped to take a breath, I asked if she would be willing to change her mind if I could prove to her that the scene we were reading was, in fact, a comedy. She (skeptically) agreed. I closed

| Connie and me | Me and Connie | Us'ns |

the script and showed her the cover, which read: *Lilacs in the Rain A Comedy in Three Acts (1955)*. The look on her face was priceless: First doubt, followed by incredulity, giving way to embarrassment, then collapsing under utter capitulation expressed by the most charming, captivating laughter I'd ever heard. I was in love and from that moment to this we've been fast friends, and sometimes even more.

What's In A Name?

It was Connie who picked a name for me that, had I taken it, would have lived forever in infamy. I'll explain. Most of the *Riot* cast lived in the vicinity of Sunset Boulevard and Laurel Canyon, a fairly famous corner. Within a three-minute walk you could find Schwabb's Drugstore, where Lana Turner was purportedly discovered, Screen Actors Guild's main office, Greenblatt's Deli, Ben Franks Cafe, Ah Fong's Chinese Restaurant, and the world-famous Chateau Marmont. These were places, except for the Chateau (too expensive), that we frequented.

One day, during a "find-a-name-for-Clarke" session, where names came up that should never be mentioned in mixed company,

Connie piped up. "I think," she said, "that the name should be something memorable. Something that reflects now. Where we are in this time and place." Connie was onto something deep and profound.

"Like what?" we all asked.

"I propose that Clarke's new name should be . . . *Ah Fong Greenblatt*, in honor of our two favorite neighborhood restaurants."

There was a great silence. And the longer the silence grew the more the idea appealed to us. Who could forget a name like Ah Fong Greenblatt?! We'd found it and loved it. Connie! Our hero! The name stuck for two weeks until Byron told us, and not very convincingly, that someone already had the name, Ah Fong Greenblatt. An actor in New York. If that was the case, we all knew the rule: If someone picks a name before you do, it's theirs.

"Gary Clarke" was born as I was boarding the bus for the first day of shooting on location. Byron was adamant. I had to pick a name, right then and there.

"Okay." I fired back. "Clarke will be my last name, and Gary will be my first. Gary Clarke! That's it!" I have no idea where Gary came from. It was probably just floating by in the ether and I grabbed it.

"Good," said Byron, and he was off to see if he could get my new name registered with SAG and get a blurb in Louella Parson's or Hedda Hopper's gossip columns. Louella came through.

FIVE – Learning the Hard Way

Dragstrip Riot was a conglomeration of many things. Bad script, bad direction, bad acting (with a few exceptions), and not enough money. There was, however, an over abundance of commitment, energy, belief in what we were doing, and perseverance. All of the actors were first-timers except for two, three counting Connie, who had just appeared in another teenage epic called *Young and Dangerous* (1955). The other two pros were Yvonne Lime who'd appeared with Burt Lancaster and Katherine Hepburn in *Rainmaker* (1956), and Fay Wray, whom you will all remember as the screaming heroine in the original *King Kong* (1933). In this film, Yvonne was my girlfriend and Miss Wray was my mom. I shouldn't have to tell you all this. You should have a copy of this gem in your film library (*Dragstrip Riot,* not *King Kong*).

I shouldn't make too much fun of this film. It was, after all, the start of many careers: Connie has made numerous films, a TV series, recordings, and created a successful cosmetic line; Tony Butala went on to form The Lettermen singing group, which is still going strong; Steve Ihnat was very successful in films and TV. Others got out of the business, but all enjoyed a modicum of success as actors. As you probably know, in most/all movie productions, there are horror stories, and sometimes those are the fun things to talk about, so. . . .

We were all signed to a three-week contract at $125 per week, *and* we all got our Screen Actors Guild (SAG) card. Now, a three-week

Fay Wray: "It's true, Rick. Your father *is* King Kong."

contract means just that: You work three weeks, you get paid for three weeks, and you move on, which is what Yvonne and Fay did. SAG says that you *do not*, under any circumstances, work beyond what your contract states, unless there is a re-negotiation and further compensation. Given that the entire budget for *Dragstrip Riot* was about four dollars, there was certainly no room for further compensation. When that's the case, and further shooting is necessary to complete the movie, then the producer, in this case, Dale, goes to work. He begins by praising our performances.

Now, when I need her, she just sits on my car, yawns and taps her toe!

"When *Dragstrip* is released," Dale said, "other producers and directors will be clamoring for your services! New, bigger and more famous agents will be fighting to sign you."

We bought it. Next, the *Setup*!

"The smartest thing I ever did was to cast you people in this movie," he said. "It already exceeds my greatest expectations! We are all going to be rich and famous!!"

And finally, the *coup de gras!* Two days later, he'd show up on the set wearing an expression that said, *My wife left me, my dog died and they stole my favorite truck.* (He loved country western music.) When he was sure we'd all noticed, he'd slink away, leaving us to our own conjectures. Another two days would pass and he'd call us into a "for-our-ears-only" meeting during which he "confided" in us. Us. His family, the only ones who would truly understand.

To Infinity And Beyond

"I'm sorry, guys. But," Dale struggles to hold back a tear, "we've run out of money. Our financiers were adamant. No more money. I pleaded with them but . . . not another penny. And we, our family, being so close to completion! It's unbear—" This time a tear did fall. "Just a little more shooting time is all we need, but I can't pay you and . . . and I won't ask you to work for nothing . . . even though I *know* you would all emerge stars, in this, the business, the profession that you love. That you've worked so hard for. Oh, I don't care about me, I can always get a job as a film editor, but you. . . . Oh, why did this. . . ."

By now we, gullible little newbies that we were, were *all* in tears, vowing that we would not let *our* movie be thwarted by the lack of some little piddly-ass thing like money! "We're with you, Dale!" we cried. "We'll show 'em! Let's do it, guys!!"

"And I promise," wept Dale. "It'll only be a week or two. Three at the most."

Six months later, when we were firmly ensnared in Dale's web, we were still shooting and in too deep to stop. And when I say six months, I do not mean an uneventful, ho-hum six months. There were a few events, call them near-death experiences, catastrophes, and *what-the-hell-am-I-doing-here* moments. Allow me elucidate:

All members of the good gang drove white Corvettes. How else would you know that we were the good guys?? There was one exception: Brad—the Judas in our gang—he drove a *grey* Corvette. Come to think of it, he also had *black* hair. Why didn't I think of that before? I digress. There was a scene that we shot on the curvy Malibu Canyon roads where five

"That's right! No one gets in with black hair!"

bikers were chasing me in my white Corvette. Dale had convinced a real biker—they called him *"Spokes"*—to get four of his friends to work with us with the promise that his "very next movie" was about a motorcycle gang and he was going to use *their* gang.

Mid-day and we're taking a break alongside one of the less traveled canyon roads. A bunch of big oak trees, rocks to sit on, sandwiches and Dr. Peppers. One thing Dale *did* do was feed us. Not well, but enough. Right next to our break area was a small hill. On it was a path where it looked like other bikers had been testing their dirt bikes. The path led up to the top of the hill, where it widened, curved and then came back down, meeting at the same spot where it started, thus making a tear-drop shape.

I was *not* a proficient biker, but I was also not one to pass up an opportunity. I "borrowed" one of the bikes and made my first run on the "tear-drop." Not too fast, but good for a novice. Let's try that one again. A little faster this time. Very, very good. I was headed for round three when Dale asked Spokes to get me off the bike for fear that some unforeseen mishap should occur. Spokes jumped on his bike and headed into the tear-drop area. Not good. As he entered, I was barreling down the back side. I saw him. He saw me. Too late. I broadsided him, hard. I heard a loud "crack!" I flew up, off my bike, over the handlebars, over Spokes and his bike, headed for some unsuspecting bush thirty feet away. Result: I scratched my finger and lost my shoe. Spokes was a different story. I broke his leg. That was the "crack" I'd heard. There was blood streaming out of his glove, and when we took it off a splintered bone was sticking out through the flesh. We took him to the hospital. They set his leg and his hand, affixing the appropriate casts, and he was back on the set the next morning.

Meanwhile, we had a problem. It had already been established that *five* bikers were chasing me, and we now only had *four* that could ride. The issue was quickly solved like this:

The camera was set up on the side of the road and locked in position so that it wouldn't move. I then drove my Corvette by the camera, making sure my face was identifiable. They shut off the camera, making sure it hadn't moved. They then lined up the four bikers, put *me* in a biker's outfit, on a bike, and when the director yelled "action," we all took off in pursuit of me. That's right. There is a shot in the film where I am actually *chasing myself.* Show biz!

Hail To The Chief

The incident that had the most impact on me resulted from a scene we were shooting late one night in a downtown Hollywood apartment building. It was just the cameraman, the sound man, Dale and me (Dale was running lights). We (Dale) chose to shoot in the wee hours because, according to Dale, "The SAG cops don't like working late. Nobody knows we're here. We'll be fine. Not to worry."

By this time, when Dale said "Not to worry," we worried. And it was justified.

Just about the time Dale was congratulating himself about how he'd out-foxed Screen Actors Guild, Screen Actors Guild walked in. Two official, polite, well-dressed middle-aged men. Think *Men in Black.* It was surreal. Like a movie within a movie. They

Jerrene and Kathleen Freeman

were there to see me! Dale tried to intervene by telling them it was a student film and he was working on his thesis and that I was just helping him out. I think the point at which he lost them was when he said he was going to make a movie about SAG and would like

both of them to star in it. With that, the sound man and cameraman began packing up. The MIB guys suggested in no uncertain
terms that it would be in my best interest to leave the site immediately and that I would hear from them shortly. Dale never knew how
close he came to death that night. Or maybe he did—he avoided me
like the plague. However, for me, the best was yet to come.

I was invited to a hearing, on my behalf, at the SAG building on
Sunset Boulevard in Hollywood. *So,* I thought, as I made my way to
my well-deserved demise. *This is what it's like to be ridden out of town
on a rail.* Yes, once again my career was over before it even began.
All that was left for me was to start over. Change my name. Find a
cheap plastic surgeon. Perhaps a sex change.

I was escorted into a large room on the second floor. There were
twenty or twenty-five chairs arranged in a semi-circle. Facing the
semi-circle was one lone chair—mine. My escort was a very nice gentleman I'd seen dozens of times in movies. He assured me that it
wouldn't be as bad as I thought. He also had no idea how really bad
my thoughts were.

The "jury" moseyed in. Many came up and introduced themselves to me. All smiling, all glad to meet me. These were actors!
I mean real actors! The lifeblood of the business! I was in awe. I
wanted to ask them all for their autographs and then thought better of it. I can't think of one name now, but I could sure point them
out if I saw them. One name I do remember: Kathleen Freeman.
You've seen her a million times. I remember her because years later
we became good friends. That was one incredible woman.

One gentleman opened the meeting and announced that the
SAG President was on his way. He talked about movie stuff and
how most everyone in the room had, at one time or another, gotten
in hot water with SAG. A ripple of laughter from the group told me
that everyone there had experienced what this man was saying. It

was about there that I began breathing again.

The president of Screen Actors Guild entered, shook my hand and introduced himself (as if I wouldn't know). Then he began to speak, so eloquently and passionately, about what the Guild had done for its actor over the years, how they had made making movies safe, how, no matter who the actor was, the Guild would always take care of them, which is why they built the Actors Home. What he said and how he said it made me want to rip off my shirt, hand him a whip, lay prostrate at his feet, and scream *"Beat me! Beat me!"* That man laid out the whole history of the Guild in a way I would never forget. That man who spoke so eloquently, the Screen Actors Guild president at that time, was Ronald Reagan.

SIX – On The Move

Looking back, it was about here that things began to move very fast. It didn't seem that way at the time, but when you're in the middle of it things never seem to go the way you'd like. Nevertheless, Byron, flying around on the coattails of *Dragstrip Riot,* procured audition after audition for me. If there was anything in which there was a character I even remotely resembled, I was there, auditioning.

One "B" movie—the name escapes me—touted a female villain, very mean, very ruthless, very pretty. Byron actually convinced the casting director that it would be a "marvelous idea" to have the villainess actually be a guy, in drag. Guess who it was that Byron touted as that drag guy? Right. The casting lady reluctantly agreed to see me "in character." Byron supervised my costuming, wig, and makeup. While I hate to admit it, I was gorgeous. The casting lady thought so, too. However, the director, who happened to be gay, did not think I looked believable. "His lips aren't pouty enough," he said. Byron countered by suggesting Collagen. I countered by leaving.

While all this was going on, I was still dealing with my personal life. Or did you think that it's all just auditions, getting parts, making big money, and seducing starlets? No. There were priorities. Eating was one. A place to sleep was another.

By now I had vacated my digs at "Byron's Hotel" and was looking. I was fairly fortunate. Two brothers, Joseph and Victor Satinsky, who had funded *Dragstrip Riot,* had taken a liking to me. Joseph was very successful in the mercantile business. Victor was a heart surgeon and the co-creator of coronary-bypass surgery. Anyway, they put me under personal contract and paid me the whopping sum on $200 per month *and* gave me a place to live.

The living quarters were two rooms in a large, empty, two-story building right on Sunset Boulevard. There was a bed, an old stove, and an even older refrigerator. And a phone!—which I had to pay for out of my $200. All-in-all, a great deal.

I know what you're thinking. You want to go by my old place and rip off a piece of sideboard, frame it and, caption it with, "Gary Clarke Slept Here." Well, too bad. A few years after I moved out, they razed the place and overnight it became a Burger King. And besides, I did the ripping off, framing, and captioning thing. Even hung it on my wall. No one ever noticed it, and if they did, they ignored it. Last time I saw it, it was leveling a table on my mother's back patio. So much for memorabilia.

SEVEN – A Fork In the Road

It was about here that my career took off on another tangent: Singing in a *big* stage show in Miami Beach. Tony Butala and another singer (forgot his name) were already cast as two of the three "Delta Rhythm Boys." That was the trio that launched Bing Crosby's career. The third member of the trio had to drop out due to another commitment, and Tony recommended me. I auditioned and got the part. The future was beginning to look rosy and then some. Until . . . I got a call from my draft board. It seemed that my (first) ex-wife had called them and painted a not-very-nice picture of me and convinced them that a hitch in the army just might straighten me out. They loved the idea. I pleaded and begged them to at least give me a three-month postponement so I could do the stage show, which might make it easier for me to get a job when I got out. Besides, I was already in the Navy Reserves. But they weren't buying. I was to report in two weeks—four days before I was to leave for Miami Beach.

Life looked bleak. For sure my career was over. I'd be thirty or thirty-one when I got out. *Old!!* Who'd want me? After relating my fate to everyone I knew, I actually resigned myself to the fact: I was in the army now! Well, almost. I was to report for duty on a Monday. The Friday before, I called to find out what, exactly, I was to bring with me. Any special color toothbrush? Were they going to give me underwear or do I bring my own? Can I bring *Pookie*, my bear?

I was talking to this guy at the Draft Board, asking everything I

Rudy Vallee   Buster Keaton   Paul Whiteman   Me

thought I should ask, when he said, "Wait a minute. Let me check something." Sixty seconds later, he came back and the news that he brought with him had me dumbfounded. I couldn't believe it! I sprouted wings, flew out my door, buzzed Sunset Boulevard, floated weightlessly back into my apartment, and landed like a feather on my Goodwill mattress.

"Clarke," he said, "Your status has been changed from 1A to 5A and you've been put on standby reserve."

"Standby Reserve?" I asked, the frog in my throat betraying me. "Does that mean I can still be called?"

"Yes," he answered. "But only if America is attacked at all four borders at the same time. Have a good time in Miami Beach."

Then he hung up. That was it. I'd been un-drafted! I have no idea how or why or who or what . . . that's not altogether true. I did have an idea. Someone had interceded on my behalf, but I never, ever, found out who, but I still say prayers for him or her or them.

Pros Plus

Miami Beach and I really liked each other. And the stage show was something else. It was called *Newcomers of 1928* (1958) and starred Rudy Vallee, Paul Whiteman, Harry Richman, Fifi Dorsey, and Buster Keaton, all of whom were *big* stars in 1928, just thirty years earlier, and were still well known. Kinda like seeing Meryl Streep in *Sophie's Choice* in 1982 and then seeing her in *The Iron Lady* in 2012. These guys were big stuff! And I got to work with them. Comedy bits. Skits. Cross-overs. I got to work with Buster Keaton!!

I think one of the best parts about being in that show was spending time with Buster at his hotel on our days off and trying to outdo each other with our comedy diving routines. He was great, and even at sixty-seven years of age, he kicked my butt. I got him on one dive, though. He was very impressed with my belly-flop off the ten-foot board and, gracious man that he was, called our competition a draw.

I was in Miami Beach with those amazing old-timers for six incredible weeks.

EIGHT – I'm on the Tube

I no sooner got back to L.A. than Byron had another audition for me. If I remember correctly, it was my first "paid" TV job: *Sky King* (1951). I played a cute, soulful little character who gets the crap beat out of him by some rough 'n tough cowboy. But my butt was saved. Not by Sky King, but by Penny, his niece, played by Gloria Winters, who was blonde, 5'3", 120 pounds, and sweet. The cowboy is beating me up, I'm spewing blood all over the place, and Penny steps in, calls the guy a "big bully," which in itself was enough to make him quake in his boots and run for the hills. But no! He does neither. It's *Penny* who proceeds to punch him out, knock him down, rip off one of his legs and beat him over the head with it, bury her foot, up to her ankle, in his butt, and tie him to the tail of a wild brahma bull that takes off like a shot and doesn't stop till it reaches Venezuela. Then, *then*, Sky King runs into the scene and, with great concern, says, "Penny! Penny! Are you alright?" Is *Penny* alright?!? Was he nuts?? I'm bleeding a quart a minute and he asks if *Penny's* okay. It was at that point I realized that not all scripts are award winners. But, what the hell? It was still a great way to earn an honest buck.

A-one-and-a-two...wait, a-two-and-a-three...

NINE – Dale and the Movies

Connie and I were still close. She got a great break (deserved), went under contract to Warner Bros., and co-starred in the TV series, *Hawaiian Eye* (1958) with Bob Conrad and Anthony Eisley. She played a singer in a Hawaiian night club who actually sang. And very well, I might add. Adorable. While Connie was doing her insignificant stuff at Warners, I was making real movies. Big time stuff. Stuff with class, like: *Missile To The Moon* (1957), *How To Make A Monster* (1957), *Date Bait* (1958), *Passion Street* (1959), *Strike Me Deadly* (1960). I could go on, but you'd only think I was bragging.

Passion Street is particularly memorable. I think it was the story-line that attracted me. That and the $300 per week they were paying me, and the free trip to New Orleans. The Story Line: I played the part of an Episcopalian minister who falls in love with and marries a prostitute while she continues to have an affair with a vice cop which prompts me to get drunk, climb the twenty-foot-high statue of Andrew Jackson situated in Jackson Square in the heart of the French Quarter, and, while on top of said statue, rip off my collar and denounce God. Now I ask you . . . what actor wouldn't jump at the opportunity to star in that movie? Oh, Dale Ireland not only directed this epic, he directed *Dragstrip Riot* and *Date Bait* as well.

Steve Ihnat and I became best friends. We had both worked on *all* of Dale Ireland's films and learned a lot about what it takes to put a movie together. Like money. Dale was a genius at raising money for movies. I don't know how he did it, but he did, time and time again. Unfortunately, he burned every bridge behind him. I think the money people he cajoled are the ones who coined the phrase, *Fool me once, shame on you; fool me twice, shame on me.*

Another thing we learned was that despite everything else, Dale liked us and looked out for us. If we were on the set and food was short, he'd forgo eating to ensure there was plenty for us. Even through all of his shady dealings, he was still one of the good guys. I look back now and am forever grateful to him. If it weren't for Dale, I might still be working at Grimley's. RIP, Dale.

You have to understand, the movie business is and always has been a feast or famine industry. Those who work a lot feast; those who don't do a lot of famining. I spent a good deal of time famining. So did Steve, and so did Dale. At one point, we were all famining together, and after thoughtful con- sideration (four minutes), we

A persistent nightmare.

decided to pool our resources so that if one of us was working, he could help sustain the other two until they got work. Unfortunately, none of us had any resources, but even *we* could figure out that 3 X 0 = 0.

Dale was the first to come through. He found us a place to live— for *nothing*! A big, two-story house, maybe seventy years old, kind of dilapidated but not bad. We were to house-sit until the owner got back from Europe, in about ten years or something like that. Dale even managed to have the realtor throw in a bunch of mattresses, a stove, and a refrigerator. Water and gas were paid, but we had to pay the electric. Perfect. Now all we needed was food. We'd all come up short in that area. Pooling our "resources," we came up with one dollar and thirty-six cents (that figure is emblazoned in my mind forever). How could we put that money to the best possible use? We calculated every way we knew, and here's what we did:

To Eat Or Not To Eat

Steve and I donned our bulkiest jackets, took $1 of our $1.36 to the local supermarket (Ralph's, I think), and shopped. I grabbed a three-pack of filet mignon steaks and a pound of butter and stuck them in my shirt under my jacket. Steve did the same with three boxes of frozen vegetables. The $1 was spent on milk and bread, with a little left over for gas (30¢ per gallon)—we all had cars. If one of us happened to pocket a candy bar or two, we had dessert. Otherwise, all that Steve and Dale had to worry about were cigarettes. I didn't smoke, so it wasn't a problem for me. We lived like that for a month, eating really quite well. Then Steve and I noticed a kind of unrest, a growing annoyance and resentment with Dale. It stemmed from the fact that Steve and I were doing all the procuring, while Dale just sat at home partaking of the fruits of our labor. He brought nothing to the table, so to speak. We talked. The more we talked, the more nervous and trepidacious Dale became. He was either going to con-tribute—something!—or starve. It was settled. Dale would accom-pany us during our next food forage and he would come away with something, *anything*, or he wouldn't eat.

Dale always wore tight-fitting bell-bottom slacks. Nice looking, pretty much the style of the day. And when I say tight, I mean Dale's were very tight. You could tell his religion through them. This is an important point because this is what he wore to our caper. Tight bell-bottom slacks and a *tee-shirt!* And he was scared. We were hoping he wouldn't pee himself until *after* we left the market.

Steve and I did our thing, feeling the necessity to distance ourselves from Dale. As we watched him, his eyes wide with fear and guilt, we fully expected him to run up to the security guard, fall at his feet, grab his ankles and scream, "I did it! I'm a thief! It wasn't my fault! It was them! They made me do it! It was all them!!" But, bless his heart, he made it to the checkout counter. We were a few customers behind him and couldn't believe what we saw. He had taken four packs of cigarettes and stuffed them into his two front pockets. I'm not saying they were bulging, but the lady in front of him warned that if he didn't stop poking her with his "thing," she would call the guard. He apologized profusely and tried to hide the salami he had also stuck down his pants. Either the checkout girl was completely blind, or she saw what Dale was trying to do, pitied him, and just let him go. Needless to say, from there on out, Steve and I did our own shopping, and Dale did his.

TEN – Gangs and the Like

I'll mention it here, though I realized it long before this—I've had an angel on my shoulder for as long as I can remember. I know what I'm about to say would never apply to any of you, but, here it is—I've done some stupid things in my day, I mean *really* stupid. Things that had me riding in the same car with the Grim Reaper—sometimes literally.

I'm ten years old, playing on my front porch one minute, then surrounded by hundreds of Mexican gang members the next. A gang war in East L.A! Knives, rocks, pipes, zip-guns (look it up) in the hands of hundreds of young guys as they race toward their enemy's "turf." Then, from the midst of the rushing mass emerged one guy about fifteen. I noticed his hair looked different. He was wearing one of those little "pig tails" that bullfighters wore. In a flash, he's up on the porch, grabbing me by the shirt, and with his face in mine asks me a very pointed question: "Where you from, cabron?" I knew what "cabron" meant, but I decided not to argue.

"I . . . live here," I squeaked. I guess he was satisfied because he let go of my shirt. However, he *did* leave me with a cryptic warning: "Hokay. Wahchit, pendejo!" I also knew what "pendejo" meant.

The next morning, I walked the three blocks to Bridge Street Grammar School. On my way, I passed Prospect Park, our small neighborhood park situated right across the street from my school. Police cars were everywhere. Ambulance lights were flashing. Uniformed cops were running all over the place. Neighbors were out en masse and school kids were trying to get a look. I squeezed through to the front to find out what all the excitement was about.

And I saw. The police were pulling two bodies out from under some bushes and laying them, a little too roughly, I thought, on two stretchers. The attendants, moving quickly to get the bodies into the ambulances, came right by me. I could have reached out and touched them. They weren't covered very well and I saw both of them. One's eyes were still open, staring at nothing. The other one had a pigtail on the back of his head, like a bullfighter. It was the kid from my front porch. They did a quick check at the ambulance then covered him up—just like in the movies. For some reason I wanted to cry.

Barbara and "The Boys"

Speaking of gangs. I'd had the opportunity to work with Louis Prima and Keely Smith at The Desert Inn in Las Vegas, which happened just before I landed the role of "Dick" on the *Michael Shayne* (1960) TV series. Louis and Keely's man-

Need I say more?

ager was a tough lady by the name of Barbara Belle who, along with her husband, Lee Neuman, took a liking to me, and when *Michael Shayne* came along, she agreed to manage me. I was starry-eyed, ecstatic. All I knew was that Barbara knew *everybody* and she wanted to manage me! When I say she knew everybody, I mean she was connected. Mob connected. You would *not* want to mess with Barbara. All the "families" knew her, as did the numerous lawyers for the "families." Her sphere of influence extended into the political arena as well. Barbara called, they answered.

I remember being in New York with Barbara and Lee. We were to have dinner at a very special Italian restaurant. One that was evidently very hard to get into. And we were to be the guests of an attorney (his name escapes me) who represented many political big wigs. He was, I discovered later, a liaison between government and the mob.

The restaurant was an old, small, dingy, unimpressive little dump. We entered from the sidewalk, down eight or ten steps and into a small room. Four large tables, two of which were occupied. On the back wall, several feet from where we would be sitting, was a large window with a very large window sill that opened into an air shaft. The window and the sill were covered with dust. The proprietor welcomed us—more accurately, he welcomed the lawyer—bowing, shaking the lawyer's hand, then showing us to the table of honor.

Next to our table was a party of eight. One of the women in that party had inadvertently laid her full-length ermine coat over one of our chairs. This pissed off the proprietor to no end. He snatched up the coat, apologized profusely to our lawyer, and flung the $20,000 wrap onto the dusty, dirty window sill. Had the window been open, who knows where the coat would have ended up? The owner of the coat came unglued. She screamed and yelled at the proprietor, threatening to sue.

Our lawyer stood (I was seated next to him) and, with the utmost charm and grace, gathered up the lady's coat, gently shook away the dust, and apologized. She snatched the coat from his hands, glowering, and sat back down in her chair, which he had chivalrously held for her. He then told the proprietor to bring the lady and her table two bottles of Dom Perignon. He handed the lady his business card and returned to our table as if nothing had happened.

The lady, still irate, had passed the business card to her husband. He looked at it and winced, his eyes bulging. He passed the card around the table, and you would have thought by their expressions that their lives were over. The husband explained to the wife, who I'm sure shat in her pants. Then, like two kids who had been caught having sex in church, they approached our lawyer and apologized in a way I had never seen. And to make a point, the woman tossed her ermine coat onto the window sill again. The proprietor grabbed it, handed it to the husband, and the entire party left, in a hurry, leaving a very large pile of cash on the table. Everyone at our table took it in stride and soon the incident was forgotten.

I had been a little queasy all day, didn't feel much like eating, and I mentioned it briefly to Barbara. Our lawyer overheard and ordered a drink for me. Something to settle my stomach: *Fernet Brancha.* A liqueur. It smelled awful, but he encouraged me to drink it down all at once, so I did. Blecchhh!! But I'll tell you, in less that two minutes, the queasiness was gone, and I enjoyed the most incredible Italian meal I'd ever had. I apologize to you for not remembering our lawyer's name, but even if I did, I certainly wouldn't put it in print without asking him first. I mean . . . well . . . you know.

Wherever we went, Barbara would introduce me to anyone of note. Movie stars, singers, musicians, Sinatra and the Rat Pack, and some folks of questionable character. They would stream in and out of her Sunset and Vine office, doing business or just dropping in to pay their respects.

"Da Mick"

It was about this time that I was having trouble with an agent who claimed to have gotten me a job. He hadn't. But he was spreading rumors that I had welched. The only way he would back off was for me to drop Byron and sign with him. I told Barbara about it. She didn't like it. She had things planned, and this kind of potential road block was an annoyance. I said it would probably all go away, and she proceeded to explain how bad publicity worked. She said she was going to make a few calls and asked me to go home and wait until I heard from her. I did. She called and asked me to meet her at her office at 6:00 the next evening. I did. We were going to see a man who could help.

Barbara, Lee, and I took a short drive into the Hollywood Hills, stopping at a gate, beyond which was a driveway that lead up to a very expensive-looking yet unassuming house. Two "men" exited the gate and approached the car, one on each side. Lee rolled down his window and the man looked in. "Hi, Barbara," he muttered. "Go on in. He's waiting for you. Is this the kid?" Barbara acknowledged that yes, I was "the kid." We passed through the gate and made our way to the main entrance, also, flanked by two more "men."

Inside, we were escorted by yet another "man" into a den or drawing room and into the presence of two more "men," and *the* man. *The* man wasn't very tall. Maybe 5'8" and a bit stocky. He was dressed in slacks, expensive slipper/shoes, a silk robe (blue?), and a white silk scarf around his neck. Everything about him was impeccable. He was at the bar sink washing his hands as we entered.

"Barbara, you look wonderful. It's been too long," he said as he hugged and kissed her. He turned his attention to Lee. "Lee. Still handsome as ever. How do you do it?" More hugging. Then he turned his attention to me. "Is this the young man you were telling me about?" Barbara said yes, I was the young man she had been talking about. He approached and extended his hand. I shook it.

"Gary, " he said with a gracious smile. "It's a pleasure. I'm Mickey Cohen."

Now, for the benefit of the younger readers: Mickey Cohen was the head mob guy for the west coast. Nothing happened there without Mickey knowing about it. In the movie *Bugsy* (1991), starring Warren Beatty, Harvey Keitel portrayed "Mickey Cohen," Bugsy Sie-

"Da Mick"

gel's closest associate. All of the "families" knew and respected/feared Mickey Cohen, and here I was shaking hands with the man.

For about two seconds, I thought it was a joke. But he wasn't wearing his "I've-just-pulled-a-joke-on-you" face. I couldn't speak. He didn't take his eyes off of me. After a very, very long silence, he smiled. Then he kind of chuckled. Then he laughed and everyone in the room joined in. I looked at Barbara and Lee and they offered no assistance. Still chuckling, Mickey said to Barbara, "You didn't tell him who he was gonna meet, did you?" Barbara, smiling at me, said that she hadn't. She thought that it would be prudent not to, you know, "In case Gary talks in his sleep."

"I *don't!*" I assured them, especially Mickey. "I would never talk in my sleep! Never!"

Everybody howled, Mickey put his arm around my shoulder, escorted me to a large sofa, and had me sit. He motioned to one of the "men," who looked at me and asked, "Pepsi okay?" I said that a Pepsi would be perfect. The next thing I knew, there was a big crystal glass full of Pepsi and ice in my hand.

"So, Barbara," said Mickey. "What can I do for you and Gary?" Barbara and I, mostly Barbara, explained the situation. Barbara told him things that even I didn't know about the agent. Mickey listened and occasionally flicked a glance at one of his "men" who nodded their understanding of what Mickey wanted. It seemed like some kind of unspoken code.

All-in-all, we were there for not more than thirty minutes. An intense thirty minutes. Especially when we got into the reason we wanted to see him. Mickey must have washed his hands three times while we were there. (Barbara told me later that he had a fetish for clean hands.) When we were done, there was a warm but quick, no-nonsense goodbye, and we were out the door, into the car, and driving off into the night. It was a long time before I finally asked, "What just happened?" Barbara and Lee laughed, and Barbara said, "You did fine, honey. Everything's going to be alright." I believed her.

And it was. I have no idea what happened, who talked to whom or if so, what was said. All I know is that the "agent" never bothered me again and, on those rare occasions when our paths crossed, he would cross the street, turn around, disappear into a nearby building, or just run. And I have to admit, it felt pretty good. Barbara set me straight.

"When you ask a favor of a man like Mickey Cohen, you are, from that moment on, obligated. And you *will* repay your debt. This favor Mickey did for *me* because we go way back. This was your freebie. If you're not ready to be obligated, never, never ask."

Gary and Pat Woodell

ELEVEN – Pat and Me

Pat Woodell was my second wife. You'd remember her from the TV series *Petticoat Junction* (1963). She played "Bobby Jo," the bookworm. The very beautiful bookworm. As two aspiring actors who were "an item," we did the usual Hollywood stuff. Kinda. Our manager, Bob Marcucci, who also managed Frankie Avalon and Fabian, would set up events for us to attend, where we'd schmooze and hobnob with fan magazine folks, producers, directors, musicians, and other actors. The fan magazine liked us, and we were always asked to do some kind of layout for them. You know, "Gary And Pat Hit The Surf," or "Gary And Pat Skiing Down The Slope Of Love," or "Gary and Pat In A Romantic Moment At The Villa Capri." We were a cute young couple in love who happened to be on successful TV shows. Of course, when I was engaged to Connie Stevens, they did the exact same fan magazine stories. Whatever sells.

Pat and I had a lot of favorite places to visit. Particularly if the food or atmosphere was special. Zup's by the Zoo was a little hot dog stand in Griffith Park that my grandpa introduced me to when I was ten. They made a skirt steak sandwich on a French roll with garlic butter the likes of which I have not been able to replicate to this day. Then there was Phillipe's, kitty corner from Union Station and two blocks down from Olvera Street (the oldest street in L.A.). Phillipe's makes the best French-dipped sandwiches in America.

Zup's is gone but Phillipe's is still there. Been there since the mid-'40s. The other place for food is The Pantry, located at the corner of 9th Street and Figueroa. They opened in 1940, and their doors have *never* been closed. Ever. Steaks, chops, ham, and eggs. One interesting aspect of The Pantry is that all of their waiters are ex-cons. The service is great and the waiters will not tolerate any behavior that might upset the dining pleasure of the patrons. More than once I've

A vision

seen them escort a "disturbance" out of the place, physically and in a hurry. My kind of service.

How Dare You, Sir!

Some favorites we liked more than others. One we really liked was a little hole-in-the-wall night club called The Peppermint West, patterned after the famous Peppermint Lounge in New York. Good live music, food if you wanted it, reasonably priced drinks, and not too rowdy. All kinds of actors would drop in, dance, sing with the four-piece band, or just hang out. The dance floor wasn't very big, about 10' x 10'. The hip-high wrought iron fence separated it from the tables and the bar. And everybody danced. Great fun.

One night, Pat and I were in the club with some friends, noshing and drinking, dancing and laughing. Ten o'clock and all was well in *The Peppermint West*. It was about then I noticed three guys enter the club. Big guys. I thought for a moment that they were tackles on a Canadian football team who had lost their way. One was carrying his drink from the last bar they'd visited. The club was only half-full, so they had no problem finding a table. They did their thing, we did ours, and soon they were forgotten.

The band started playing some funky blues number, one that Pat and I both liked, so she and I and another couple hit the dance floor. If I remember correctly, Pat and I had been to some publicity event and were dressed accordingly. She was in tailored slacks and a silk blouse. I was wearing a sport coat and tie. As we rocked out, I'd noticed that the Big Guy with his "drink" had moved up to the railing and was leering lasciviously at the lady dancers, one hand draped over the railing, and one delivering occasional sips of his drink to his mouth. I also noticed, now that I had a closer view, that he was as tall sitting down as I was standing up. Then it happened. I spun Pat out a little too close to him, he couldn't resist, so he reached out and pinched her on the butt. I didn't see the pinch, but I saw the look on her face. And something snapped.

Let me digress for a moment to let you know that I will go way out of my way to avoid a fight. Walk, run, drive, or hitchhike. I will do whatever it takes to flee from a fight. Most of the time. But other times I just don't care who or what, I will walk right into it. I think it has something to do with insanity or stupidity. This was one of those times when both elements were firing on all cylinders.

I started for the Big Guy, who was just sitting there, leering and licking his chops. Pat knew better than I that this huge hulk could snap my back like a twig, and tried to steer me in the opposite direction—*by grabbing my tie and pulling.* She let go when she noticed my face turning from red to purple. She backed away and I moved boldly to confront the masher.

One hand, the hand that offended, still hung over the railing. It looked more like a ham than a hand. But, undaunted, I forged ahead. I squared up in front of him, noticing that he had yet to look at me. He was looking at Pat. It was time to really put the fear of God in him, so I leaned in and, in my toughest adrenaline-filled soprano voice, said, "A guy can lose teeth like that!" I guess he didn't hear me because he, still not looking at me, said, "What?" I started to repeat myself and got as far as, "A guy. . . . " when his huge, offending, ham-like paw swung upward and back-handed me across the face, hard enough to send me back a step.

Another slight digression: I had had maybe two-and-a-half karate lessons, so I don't know how accurate it would be to say that my karate instincts kicked in, but something akin to that happened. I found myself in front of him (he was now looking at me), my left arm across my chest, fist clenched, my right hand pulled back to my right hip, fist clenched, fingers up. And without hesitation I fired my right fist at his face, hand turning over as it went. The contact was perfect: striking with the first and second knuckles and not the third and fourth (they're more likely to break), I hit him hard enough to knock him and his chair back a few feet. I was aware of nothing else. Just him. Not Pat. Not my friends. Not the other patrons. I was watching him. I was riveted.

He stood up. And up. And up. And I, like a dummy, moved toward him. When I was in range I fired another shot. Same way. Same place. Except a little higher, now that he was standing. And again I connected. He went down, and I remember thinking, "If he gets up I'm moving to Iceland!" He didn't. But, no sooner had he hit the floor than two cops were on us. One was on the big guy, the other had me pinned up against the bass drum with his nightstick. My hero! I wanted to kiss him on the lips.

Everyone in the club came to my defense, yelling that it was the Big Guy who had started it all. A few minutes later they'd gotten the whole story and hauled the Big Guy and his two friends away. People must have heard my heart beating because many came up to me and inquired as to my well being. After confirming that everything was okay, Pat and I returned to our table and things began to settle. Still concerned, she brought me an ice pack for my hand and one for my face and kept asking if I was okay. Finally, when she was certain that everything was copacetic, she excused herself, went into the ladies room, and threw up.

As for the Big Guy, I found out about a week later that I had broken every bone in his facial mask and he was suing the club for everything he could get. For some reason, my name wasn't mentioned in the complaint. Never knew why. The judge threw out the case after the first five minutes. Evidently, Big Guy was a known international hit man who had been wanted for nine years by the FBI, the CIA, and Interpol, and had assassinated seventeen heads of state around the world, and was in L.A. to carry out his newest contract, which was to take out every single member of the *Bonanza* cast. All right. All right. I made up the part about the hit man. But I had you for a second there, didn't I?

TWELVE – Where It All Began

I am one blessed soul. I have angels. One on each shoulder. A little tired and worn out, but they're there. I can't "prove" it, but that's okay. While I'm not saying that my childhood was miserable or horrendous, it did have its scary moments. There were things that happened that could have snuffed out my innocent young life in the blink of an eye. Incidents and situations that could have taken me out without so much as a by-your-leave. Some instinct or unseen hand always managed to steer me out of harm's way. Even the path I took through my late teens and early twenties seemed somehow guided by what people might euphemistically call a determined, unwavering something-or-other. Call it what you will. For me, it's God, and I say I am *still* walking with angels.

White Bread To Tortilla

My mother and father were divorced when I was ten and my brother, Pete, was two. My mom, Pete, and I were going to share Grampa Solomon's house. True, it was a house and not an apartment like I'd always lived in, but it was divided down the middle, with a long narrow bathroom across the back that we were going to share. Like a duplex with a common bath. A kind of regular house but . . . strange. It was old, dirty, nothing matched, and it smelled bad. The whole neighborhood smelled bad. At least it smelled different. My mother said the house was about fifty years old. I guessed a hundred. I think

Grampa built it on weekends out of corrugated tin, apple crates, and cement. In any event, like it or not, this was our new home.

We'd moved from the Wilshire District, a predominately Anglo neighborhood. Grampa's house was in the middle of Boyle Heights, a predominately Chicano neighborhood in a section of Los Angeles about a mile east of Union Station and Olvera Street. The way my mother was acting, you would've thought she'd lived in this make-shift, discombobulated firetrap forever. I was holding Pete and my mother was unloading boxes. Pete, laughing and wriggling, couldn't have cared less. He was only two! What'd he know?

This new "home" of mine was on Fairview Avenue, a block from Brooklyn Avenue, which ran through the center of Boyle Heights, across Soto Street, and up into City Terrace.

Fairview was a short hill. One block, two houses on our side of the street, and two on the other. Grampa's house was built right off the sidewalk. With its up-hill side on the ground and its down-hill side propped up by six-by-sixes on cement pilings, it seemed to defy all laws of gravity.

Bernardo "Kid" Solomon

I was peeking cautiously through one of several crawl holes, marveling that I could see all the way to the back yard, when I saw my first rat! It may have been a mouse, but it was a rat to me. It scur-ried expertly through a vast labyrinth of spider webs and vanished silently into a black recess of the mysterious underside of the house. I wondered how long it might be before it found me in my bed and ate my eyeballs.

Then there were the steps. Seven cement steps leading from the sidewalk up to the cement porch. They were all different sizes. Narrow, wide, tall, short, passively daring me to climb or descend without falling on my butt. Many fell; I didn't. Not once in the five years we lived there. No mean feat.

Grampa Solomon was one of the most unforgettable characters I ever met. In 1907, he fought a guy named Abe Atell for the lightweight championship of the world. They went twenty rounds, wearing those lightweight gloves they used to wear, and after what was called "a hell of a fight," Grampa lost by decision. He always claimed he was drugged. Not as a complaint; just as a matter of fact. I eventually met a few of his old cronies, and they all confirmed the drugged claim. I believed him. Especially after hearing about some of the beatings he'd given others in the ring. Also, I think the drug story has a lot more oomph to it than just, "Oh, yeah. I lost."

Comes The Dawn

The guys in my neighborhood, about eight of us, always hung out together. I was the only Caucasian. I'm half-Mexican but looked like a *gringo*. Still do. One of our favorite pastimes was playing football on a residential street right behind my house. We liked this particular street because there were never any cars parked in front of the

Clarke and Pete   "Los dos gringos in East L.A."

houses, and on the corner was this little "mom and pop" store run by the parents of Alex, one of the guys who hung out with us. We'd play for an hour or two, take a break, go into the store, and each buy a small carton of milk and a package of two Hostess cupcakes, chocolate with chocolate icing, for a nickel. These weren't just ordinary cupcakes. They had this creamy choco-latey-ness that no other cupcake came close to. Couple that with a carton of ice-cold milk! Heaven!

We'd take our goodies, go across the street, sit on a neighbor's lawn under the big, leafy tree, eat, and tell jokes and stories. Ones we'd recently heard and old ones worth repeating. When we ran out of those, we'd make up stories about things we'd seen or done – mostly exaggerated. *This* was the really fun part. We'd sail off into flights of fantasy, weaving our tales of battling super villains, win-ning the race against all odds, finding a sack of gold coins or finding a "Jap spy" and helping the FBI capture him.

However, there was one subject that would, no matter who initi-ated it, always command our rapt attention: *Sex!* It's important to understand here that we were all between eleven and thirteen, and even though we'd read all the words and seen most of the pictures, we hadn't a clue. Vivid imaginations, yes. But utterly clueless when it came to the intimacies between men and women.

Invoking the former and ignoring the latter, we would regale each other with fantasies we vowed were the absolute truth. Trysts and liaisons with one or more of the most beautiful neighborhood wives; a dalliance with the prettiest girl in school and/or the petti-est teacher; or meeting a lonely army wife in the movies and making out during the entire double feature, newsreel, and cartoon. Impera-tive: the stories had to have at least a semblance of believability to them. The truth be known, had *any* of us had, at that time, found ourselves in a romantic setting with a lovely, amorous, experienced female with lust in her eyes, we would have, immediately after pee-ing our pants, run for the hills screaming, "Mommie! Mommie!"

I wouldn't have missed those story-telling sessions for the world. Those were some of the special times of my youth. It was also a time that changed my path in life forever.

I mention this because it was at this time, on this very lawn, that I discovered that I could make people laugh and that I loved doing it. It not only made others feel good but me as well. It also made me feel safe, and wanted, and like I belonged. I remember Alex saying in his thick, *vato* accent, "Hey, Clarkie! Jou're funny, man! Jou could make a lot of money making people laugh!" That was it. That was the moment. It was as if the angel on my shoulder whispered in my ear. *Listen to the young man, Clarke. This is for you.* The fun of it all became an integral part of my life from then on. So much so that fifty years later, Jerrene said that she wouldn't marry me unless I wrote in our marriage vows that I would always bring humor to our relationship. I did and it's worked. We are more in love now than we ever were. Think about it: don't you always feel better when you're having a good laugh? You know, the kind where you're laughing so hard you can't catch your breath? It's one of God's gifts to me, and it's only kept alive by sharing it. So I do. As a famous Jewish mom once said, "Try it. You'll like it."

THIRTEEN –
Bridge Street School

Lucy And The Gringo

One more life-altering incident during that period of my life. Bridge Street Elementary School was like no school I'd known before. I was ten years old and in the fifth grade. But there were guys in my class who were fifteen, sixteen, and seventeen. Grown men! To me, anyway. So what were they doing in the fifth grade? I learned that there were "Truant Officers" patrolling the streets. If they found a kid or, in the case of the "kid/guys" in my class, skipping school, they got one chance. Just one. Get caught again, and you'd find yourself in reform school. The kid/guys in my class called themselves "pachukos" or "Zoot Suiters." Today they're called "gang-bangers."

Some of the "girls" in my class weren't exactly "girls." They were full-blown women. Several were *pachukas,* the female version of *pachukos.* The *pachukas'* dress was a little different from their male counterparts: Black or brown flats, ankle socks, usually white, a well-fitted blouse or sweater, and tight, short skirts. Short enough so that if you were looking from the right angle you could see all the way to Bakersfield.

Their hair was worn about shoulder-length and was usually accompanied by very high pompadours where they secreted away things like small knives and razor blades. I had heard the stories, and it wasn't long before I was able to affirm them.

Lucy was a *pachuka*, and nobody messed with her. Boys and girls alike. I guessed she was about sixteen. A seasoned sixteen. I once saw her punch and kick a kid all the way down the stairs from the third floor to the first. He'd made some crack about the "vato" in the "charp car" that occasionally picked her up after school.

Lucy didn't pay me too much mind. I was just a "punk kid." But she did hang a name on me that some of the other kids called me from time to time: *Gringo Salado.* "Salty American." Doesn't sound like much, but it was, for *wedos* (white guys), a major put-down.

I should probably say here that I was either exceedingly naïve or as dumb as a doorknob. There were fights all the time. Gang wars. Knifings. "Zip gun" shootings. Muggings. And more. And I wandered through all of this more or less as a matter of course. But, after a while, the "gringo salado" label got to me. Lucy! If I could just get Lucy to stop, then maybe the other kids would stop. One of my friends asked me why I didn't give her a "chop", the then term for "verbal put-down." So I asked, "Like what?" He suggested a rather eloquent one which I practiced over and over during the next few weeks. My friend said that this Mexican comeback would be the best "chop" ever.

With absolutely no thought of any repercussion, I learned the saying perfectly (by now my accent was superb). I was ready for anyone, particularly Lucy. Then, nothing happened. Everyone, coincidentally, stopped referring to me as "el gringo salado." They were all on to more interesting things. After a couple of months, I'd pretty much forgotten the whole thing. Oh well, the best laid plans. . . .

Then one day, as I was sitting in my front row seat, Lucy came into class and headed for her back row seat (smart ones sat up front, incorrigibles in the back). As she passed she let me have one: "Orale!

Gringo salado!" and kept on going. Without giving it a single thought I turned in my seat and shot right back at her, "Si, pero tu quieres hacer muy Americana con el culo prieto!" Roughly translated: "Yes, but you're trying to be an American with your ass black."

The whole class hooted and hollered and made that "Oooo" sound that means "He got you that time, baby." Lucy was simmering and others added fuel to the fire. "He really chopped your ass, Lucy!" Most thought it was cool and funny.

"Atta way, Clarkie."

"Hey. The gringo strikes back."

"He talks more better than you, pachuka."

Lucy turned to look at me and I was sure I heard the "chink" of knives and razor blades coming from her hair. She moved toward me, I streaked for the door, and ran headlong into Mrs. Benton, our matronly teacher. She grabbed me by the scruff, glowered and asked me where I was going. I stammered a bit. I must have look scared, because her expression softened. She looked at me, then at the class, then back to me.

"Is someone threatening you, Clarke?" The class was breathless, waiting to see if I was going to squeal. I knew better. Squealing meant I would have to deal with Lucy *and* her friends. Not squealing and I would just have to deal with Lucy. I said, "Sorry, Mrs. Benton, but I got diarrhea."

The class roared, Mrs. Benton let me loose and I was off to the lavatory. Happy to say there were no repercussions. Turns out I made the right choice by not squealing. Lucy and I never became pals, but she did evidence a modicum of respect for me. No one ever called me "gringo salado" again, either. It was clearly one of those occasions where I could have just as easily turned up in Prospect Park beaten to a bloody pulp, or worse. Don't tell *me* God doesn't assign guardian angels!

Movie poster for *Missile to the Moon* c. 1957

FOURTEEN –
Post *Dragstrip Riot*

I'm reluctant to give you this next piece of information for fear of turning you completely against the entertainment industry forever. Just know that, as hard as it is for you to believe, I speak the truth. And the truth is that after the successful production and release of *Dragstrip Riot,* there was *not* a rash of calls clamoring for my services as an actor. My mailbox was not stuffed with contracts for me to sign. Not one word from MGM, Paramount, Warner Bros., Universal, any of them! One consensus was that the important people in the industry had not yet seen *Dragstrip Riot.* The other consensus was that they had. Either way, I was not about to be stymied or stopped. I would prevail. After all, Ronald Reagan had his *Bedtime for Bonze* (1951), Steve McQueen had his *The Blob* (1958), George Clooney had his *Return to Horror High* (1987), I had my *Dragstrip Riot.* The perseverance paid off. Byron (my agent) got a call from an independent producer! They wanted me for a sci-fi epic called *Missile to the Moon*!!

Girls, Girls, Girls, And Some Rocks

A fascinating story. "Dirk," a scientist, builds a spaceship in his back yard—hidden from the prying eyes of his nosy neighbors—with the intention of flying to the moon. We don't know that he's already been there once and just *has* to get back. He enlists the help of his friends,

Steve and June, who didn't have anything planned for the weekend anyway. They're short-handed but they're going to go for it. They pay no attention to the news blurb about two convicts who'd just escaped from a nearby prison. (This is where Tommy Cook and I come in.)

NOTE: My name in the movie was "Lon." My convict partner's name was "Gary." "Why," I asked, "don't we change names? Avoid any confusion." A few scathing looks and the matter was dropped. I was "Lon" and that was that. Oh, one other point of interest: This entire film was to be shot in seven days. That sounded familiar.

We, the convicts, sneak on board the rocket ship and stow away in the cargo bay (where else would we stow?) and off we go. I have often wondered why the neighbors never complained about the noise. Some time later, "Gary" and I are discovered in the hold just seconds before death would have claimed us, and we're shanghaied for the rest of the trip. We brought up the possibility of turning around, but it seemed there were only two choices: Stay on board and go to the moon, or take our chances with parachutes. "Gary" and I opted for the full lunar excursion. And before we knew it, we were there.

We land, don our space suits (they had two extras that just happened to fit "Gary" and me), exit the ship and follow Dirk as he heads for "the cave" that will lead us to his big surprise and the "treasure." Yeah, treasure. Dirk had accidentally spilled the beans about there being big mountains

"Aw, c'mon, Gary. It's my turn to play the tall guy."

Scene from *Missile to the Moon* c. 1957

of diamonds on the moon. He also issues a word of caution. "On our short trek to the cave be careful, be very careful." "Gary" and I wonder, *We're on the surface of the moon, we're wearing space suits, what could possibly go wrong?*

Just this. One of the walls of one of the moon mountains comes to life. "Rock Men," who only seconds before had been a part of the mountain, break loose from their pebble prison and lumber menacingly toward us. That's right: guys made out of rock (that looks suspiciously like Styrofoam) who want to chase us into the direct sunlight where we would fry like fajitas.

But, as fate would have it, and because we're only ten minutes into the movie (too soon to kill us off), we escape into "the cave" and safety, or so you would think. Just as we begin to catch our breath and our eyes adjust to the gloom, a vision appears. A beautiful young

Misses Universe in *Missile to the Moon* c. 1957

lady! As Dirk opens his mouth to speak she pulls out a Green Hornet look-alike gas gun, gives us a blast, and we're out for the count.

When we come to, we're in a large room that looks like the set for a bad high school version of *The King and I* (1956). It's at this point that we finally discover the *real* reason Dirk wanted to brave this loony lunar landing. The room is filled with gorgeous women! FYI: These women were *all* of the Miss Universe contestants of 1957. No, that's not quite true. Not all. Just the ones who weren't working at the time.

Now I can't be certain of this part, but I have it from reliable sources that their costumes came from Frederick's of Hollywood. For those of you not familiar with Frederick's of Hollywood, allow me to bring it into perspective. If Victoria's Secret is post grad, Frederick's is Pre-K. So there they were, twenty Miss Universe contestants, all fetchingly garbed and lounging. Just lying around reading *Cosmo* and *Playgirl* as if waiting for a photo shoot. And not one Moon Man anywhere to be seen. The plot thickens.

"Lido," the big kahuna, is an attractive Moon Lady but a bit longer in the tooth than the others. It seems that during Dirk's last visit, he made a deal with Lido to come back, bring a few guys and do "whatever they could" to keep the moon species alive. Well, "Gary" and I were all for helping out. At least I was. "Gary" was more interested in the diamonds (the fool!).

Suffice it to say, "Gary" bought it. He was trying to carry off too many diamonds and couldn't outrun the styrofo—I mean, the "Rock Men." They chased him into the sunlight, where he became the first fried moon bacon. My love interest, Leslie Parish, lost her life trying to save me from a big spider on wires, and Dirk stayed with Lido and tried to ride out the moonquake that was about to decimate everything. Steve, June, and I made it. I had to make it because they needed me to throw a couple of levers at just the right time. Stellar work. Lift off, and home. Hope I didn't spoil anything for you.

"Now Gary. A wolf is a wolf is a wolf."
Between scenes during *How to Make a Monster* c. 1958.

FIFTEEN – Busy, busy, busy!

By now, Connie and I were an item. Sometimes we were going steady, sometimes we weren't talking. Mostly we were fine. The fan magazines loved us, studios would get us tickets to major events, things were moving along swimmingly. By now I'd done a few more epics, all of which I'm sure you have in your film libraries. I'm talking about these:

Ya Gotta Do What Ya Gotta Do

In *How To Make A Monster*, I play an actor who plays a werewolf who falls under the spell of an evil makeup man who smears my face with hypnotic evil makeup and makes me bite out the throats of all the studio executives because they decide to stop making monster films. A ridiculous premise if ever I heard one. However, the *last ten minutes* of the film, when the makeup man gets his comeuppance, is all in *color*! I fully expected to see Dorothy and Toto being chased by tiny little people with funny voices singing something about a dead witch.

Date Bait. What can I say? Two seventeen year-olds, wanting desperately to get married. Her mommy and daddy say no, and my big brother doesn't give a poop either way. Then, a drug-driven twerp who has the hots for *my* girl threatens me and anyone in the vicinity that he will tell his big-shot gangster brother and then . . . well . . . just you wait and see. Now for the big surprise twist ending: Twerp

Me and Steve Ihnat in *Date Bait* c. 1958

dies in a shootout with his own brother, the brother is arrested—bringing down his whole gang in the process. My big brother now gives a poop. My girl's mommy and daddy see the error of their ways, realize what an excellent fellow I am, and smile affectionately as the sunset beckons us. "Our daughter is so lucky."

Strike Me Deadly, formerly titled *Crosshair,* was shot entirely in Bend, Oregon. Why? Because the producer, Ted Mikels, who hocked his house, car, wife, and kids to finance this epic, lived there. Determined, he shuffled off to Hollywood, hired me, Steve Ihnat, and an adorable newcomer, Jeannine Riley, as his stars. He also hired a cameraman, Brad Bradbury, and, with his team in tow, took us all up to the forest terrain of Bend. The plot: Jeannine and I are newlyweds and decide to use our honeymoon time to make a few bucks as Forest Rangers.

During my rounds through the forest, I happen to spot Steve killing a rival. He spots me spotting him, and the chase is on. He has a gun; I don't. I tried throwing my binoculars at him, but it just made him madder. But it wasn't all running. After all, what is a for-

Movie poster for *Strike Me Deadly* c. 1959

est ranger without a fire? So we threw in a forest fire, stock footage, of course.

There's another immensely interesting and fascinating fact about this movie: every resident in the town of Bend appeared in the

Jeannine Riley fails to teach me how to use chopsticks.
A scene from *Strike Me Deadly* c. 1959

film. Speaking parts, non-speaking parts, walk-byes, crowd scenes. If you knew anyone who lived in Bend at the time, you can be sure they showed up somewhere in the film. Even Lee Newman, my manager's husband, who drove Steve, Jeannine, and me from Hollywood to Bend, had a part. Oh, I almost forgot: My younger brother, Mike, had a part. In fact, he was the hero of the piece. He was about fourteen or fifteen at the time and drove up from L.A. with Barbara Belle.

Steve and I would rewrite the script as we went. Work a day, back to our digs, eat, then write the scenes for the next day. We were looking for an ending and decided to use Mike. And what we didn't write we ad-libbed. We may not have been good, but we were resourceful.

SIXTEEN – Buds To The End

"Alas, Poor Yorick . . . ."

During the time when I was first under contract to Universal, it also was a time when Steve was getting a lot of work, so we splurged and got an apartment together. Two bedrooms. Two baths. We flipped for bedrooms. I won and got the queen-size bed; Steve got the twin.

Steve was a Shakespeare "maven" and would go to any length to see something by the Bard. Theater, movie, television, a reading in a bar, he didn't care. He was there. His especial favorite was *Hamlet*.

On this one particular evening the BBC was presenting The Royal Shakespearian Theater's production of *Hamlet*. A big deal for avid Shakespearianites, of which Steve was a card-carrying member. There was no way he was going to miss this show. Unfortunately, he had a job and couldn't get off till 5:30. The show started at 6:00, and he was forty-five minutes away in decent traffic. He needed my help. He was going to see if he could sneak out a few minutes early, then race recklessly through traffic, and get home as close to 6:00 as possible. All he wanted me to do was turn on the TV so it would warm up (this was early '60s! TV's had to warm up!). Then when it was warmed up, I was to tune it in to the appropriate channel and make sure *everything* was the way it was supposed to be. So I did it. No big deal.

Steve hit the door about 6:01. The credits were still scrolling. Perfect! He sat on the couch. No, not *on* the couch, on the *edge* of the couch. Eyes glued to the perfectly tuned in BBC presentation of *Hamlet*, he took off his jacket, his shoes and socks and settled in. He was in "Bard heaven."

Steve Ihnat: "Do not gaze at me thus, thou addled butt-munch!"

I enjoyed Shakespeare, but not at Steve's level. So while he watched, I did other stuff. I do remember that I was hungry, and I was in the process of making tea and toast with peanut butter and honey. Gracious person that I am, I asked Steve if he would like some. It took four queries before he answered.

"Huh?" he finally muttered. "Oh. Yeah. Okay." His eyes never left the TV.

Now even though we knew that honey doesn't spoil, we kept it in the refrigerator anyway, which made it thicker and not easily spreadable.

I didn't get the idea until I was actually spreading the honey on the peanut-buttered bread. I noticed that the honey, unless I spread it with the knife, would just sit there in a glob, unmoving. The result of cold temperature on honey. I spread Steve's toast with honey that was nearly an inch thick. A perfect glob of honey spread with perfection to each edge of the perfectly toasted honey wheat bread.

I handed him his cup of tea, which he took in one hand, and then the peanut butter and honey toast, which he took in his other hand. It was all instinct because he never looked away from *Hamlet* once. I'm not sure, but I think I heard a barely audible "Thanks" somewhere in there. He was gone. Nothing short of a fire or a power outage would have moved him from that sofa.

I retreated into the kitchen to observe my handiwork from afar. It didn't take long. He took a bite, then a sip of tea, never looking at either. Another bite, another sip. He set his toast on his cup so that he could lick a drop of honey that had inadvertently reached a finger. Nature was taking its course. The room temperature and the heat from his tea made for, how should I say, a more relaxed honey. It began to move, creeping silently and slowly over the edges of the bread, a drop or two even reaching the palm of Steve's hand.

But, if nothing else, Steve was a multi-tasker. With great deftness, he would catch the renegade honey drops with a well-aimed tongue, still, never averting his eyes. And the more the honey "relaxed" the more it seemed to want to escape. And it did. Off the sides of the bread. Onto the palm and through the fingers. Steve's tongue (unbeknownst to Steve's brain) worked frantically to stem the escaping tide of the stickiest, gooiest substance God ever created.

Steve held his own for several minutes, but when the succulent nectar began running down his arm and dropping onto his feet, the end became inevitable. And what was I doing all this time? I'll tell you what I was doing. I was laying on the kitchen floor laughing my ass off, stuffing dishtowels in my mouth to avoid being heard. I just couldn't hold it any longer when I heard, exploding from the other room: "Son of a bitch!!! What the f---?!? GARY!!!" That was my cue to run! Had Steve caught me, I'm sure this story would have a different ending. But he didn't. He kept slipping on the honey.

SEVENTEEN – The Groups

Casinos Galore

When I wasn't acting or writing, I'd look for other ways to make ends meet, and it usually involved singing. Connie sang, Tony Butala and Jimmie Blaine sang, I hung out with all three of them, so singing was always a possibility. A very nice phase of my career was about to happen. Tony had met a gentleman by the name of Bill Norvas, who'd had a very successful singing group several years earlier called Bill Norvas and the Upstarts. Personal issues forced him to disband it, and now he was looking to create the group again. Tony and I auditioned with two lovely young ladies that Bill had found, Audrey Allen and Laurie Mattis. He said later that as he listened to us singing his tight, four-part harmony, he knew he'd found what he was looking for.

Bill had an incredible ear and wrote arrangements that would knock your socks off. He'd write for duos, trios, four and five-part harmony, and we'd sing them all. When we were ready, the group auditioned for the owner of the Desert Inn Hotel in Las Vegas, Nevada (can't believe I forgot his name). He thought we were terrific and gave us a try-out booking at the Wagon Wheel Hotel in Lake Tahoe right on the California/Nevada border. We were backed by piano, bass, drums, and guitar. Jimmy Blaine played bass. We opened and they loved us. What was notable for me about this club date was that it was the first time I ever sang solo in front of anyone.

Tony Butala, Audrey Allen, Bill Norvas, Lori Mattis and me
The 5 members of *Bill Norvas and the Upstarts* c. 1958

I had an idea and ran it by Bill. He said give it a shot, so I went for it. Our piano player, Vince Morton, and I got together and put together a rendition of "Mack the Knife," and it was sounding pretty good. *Hey!* I thought. *This just might work!* Bill put the number in the show that night. I was pumped. It was time. Bill gave me a nice, light introduction, I stepped forward and Vince started the vamp. But when it came time for me to sing I couldn't hear what my note was. The chord was perfect. I just didn't know what note to pick. I was all over the place, trying to cover by "talk singing." When it looked like the end, Tony and the girls started singing with me. That worked. I got on track, they doo-wopped behind me and the audience went right along with it. Bill and the group couldn't stop laughing.

Between sets (we had six shows a night) Vince and I got together to solve my problem. "What if," I ventured. "What if you just give me a bell tone? Just one note? So when I start 'Oh the shark has . . .' you just play the note for 'Oh . . .' I'll sing that and we're on our way." Vince agreed, and we were set.

On stage. My time. Bill introduces. I step forward and Vince plays. My single note is very clear and I hit it perfectly. Except . . . I was an octave too high! I was singing in the stratosphere. The whole group joined in, including the band, until I was back on track. But, that was the last time I had a problem with "Mack the Knife."

We were together for a while and, as is wont to happen, people move on. That's what Tony and I did. He was working on putting together his own trio and eventually did. You may have heard of them: The Lettermen. That's Tony's group, and it's still going strong today. He did music; I did some acting.

Several months later, Tony, Jimmie, and I were back in another group and booked into The Stardust Lounge on the Strip in Las Vegas. Eddie Lawrence was the leader. A good musician who played a great sax.

Besides Eddie, there were the standard piano, bass, and drums. Jimmie was back playing the bass. The Stardust Lounge was a very interesting place to play. It offered 24-hour entertainment. We'd do forty-five minutes, then the next group would come on and do their forty-five minutes until we'd each done six shows. Here's how that worked: It was a revolving stage. As the group before us was finishing their set, we would take our places on the back half (unseen) of the stage. The group onstage would begin playing "Stardust" and we, backstage, would begin playing as well. The stage would revolve as both groups played "Stardust," and when we were out front and the other group was backstage and out of sight, they stopped and we began our show.

The stage was directly over the bar. In fact, step off the front of the stage and you're standing in the bar well with the bartenders. I did that once. They asked me not to do it again. I didn't. The bar itself wrapped around the stage, giving customers an up close and personal view of the shows. Almost close enough to touch. Beyond the bar were twenty or thirty tables that still gave people a good shot at what was going on onstage. Beyond that, the gaming tables.

We were booked there for seven weeks, and during that time, we attracted regulars that would come back to see us time and time again. The bosses liked that. And from our vantage point, we were privy to a wide variety of drama that was always taking place in the casino. One night, after our first set, we spotted a pair of young new-lyweds celebrating their marriage and playing roulette like it was going out of style. We'd do a set, take a break, and there they'd be.

By the time we'd finished for the night, they'd lost $50,000, the new car her parents had given them, *and* the deed to the house his parents had bought for them. Friends and even the Pit Boss tried to get them to stop, but the slide was greased. They phoned home for bus fare.

On the other side of the coin we saw this plain-looking elderly man at the crap table, his plain-looking elderly wife standing by his side. By the time we had done all of our shows, they had won over $450,000. Someone asked them what he was going to do with the money. "Ten percent to the Lord, then I'm gonna pay off my ranch. But first we gotta buy Patsy a new dress." There are 10 million stories in the naked city. . . .

Fatal Attraction

Speaking of customers who came back to see us again and again. . . .

There was this one woman, maybe twenty-eight or thirty, who was there most every night and for every show. She was an exuberant audience to say the least. She'd giggle and squeal, make requests and send us tips. She struck me as the stereotype for a grammar school teacher from Boise. Glasses. Hair up in a bun. Clothes on the dowdy side. But still, attractive. It didn't take us long to realize that I was the apple of her eye, the object of her affection, the one she was there to see. And I, shameless hussy that I was, milked it for all it was worth. All of us on stage had someone like that in the audience at some point during our shows. We'd flirt, kibitz, and joke with everyone. Most women would swoon dead away when Tony sang "Maria" from *West Side Story* (1957). I'd get a few with "Mack the Knife." Sometimes there was even a *guy* who watched us with glassy eyes. But nothing ever came of them. Honest.

But the lady with the bun in her hair? That was a horse of a different color altogether. It was common for customers and performers to talk back and forth as long as it didn't interfere with the show. In fact, we included it. Everybody loved it.

"Hey, kid. I'll buy you a drink when you're finished," was one that customers said a lot. Only on rare occasions would we take anyone up on their offer. It could get complicated. By now, the young woman in question had become a permanent fixture, and it was beginning to look like she wanted my head on her wall. I asked one of the bartenders who she was (bartenders know everything). He said her father owned Las Vegas' only TV station and five big houses in and around the city, all with swimming pools. *Hmmm,* I mused, then thought better of it. Complications.

One night she was particularly aggressive and motioned several times that she wanted me to join her for a drink during my next break. We were in the middle of a number and I did something that indicated I would. Like we did to everybody. By break time, I'd forgotten the incident and joined Tony, Eddie, and the girls in the coffee shop for a snack. Break's over, we're backstage getting ready to go on, when who should show up but . . . hair bun. She wasn't happy. Ignoring everyone else, she confronted me.

"I waited for you," she said icily. "I even ordered you a drink. You didn't show. You stood me up."

My mind was racing. "Oh, I'm so sorry. I thought you meant later . . . we had to . . . we were working on some new. . . . "

"I'm here every night just to see you," she went on, oblivious to anything I had to say. "Do you know that my ultimate fantasy is to die with you in one of my father's pools?"

Tony, Eddie, Jimmie were out the door and dragging back the first security guard they could find, and not at all fast enough for me.

"Hi, Sylvia," says the guard. He knows her. "I've told you before, you can't come backstage while the shows going on. C'mon. Let's go."

As he escorted her out she turned back and left me with, "Any of my dad's pools." We watched as he escorted her through the casino, to the front door and out. It was only then that any of us felt like laughing about it. Okay. Crisis over and we're back on stage doing what we do. It was going very well. The infusion of extra adrenaline? Maybe.

Then the audience started laughing. And not at a place where they usually laughed. Even the bartenders were laughing. Was my fly unzipped? Is one of the girls exposed? Then we began to hear a "Pssst!" sound. "Pssst!" There it was again. Like a short gas leak. I looked at Tony. He pointed to the curtain behind me. I looked. It was Sylvia, peeking through the curtain, "Pssst"-ing!

"Die with me! Die with me!!" Connie's brother, Chuck, had a similar run-in with the same lady a year later.

Oh, Security!!

EIGHTEEN – Revue Studios

Not long after I got back from Vegas, I had an audition at Revue Studios for *Michael Shayne, Private Detective*, which they taped, and a few days later I had the part. What I heard was that there were three guys up for the part. The two in-house directors, Robert Florey and Paul Stewart (the two who would direct all of the shows) were in the viewing room watching all the audition tapes. When the three had been shown (mine had been shown first), the producer, who was sitting in the back of the room, asked, "Well, who is it?" Without saying a word each director raised a hand with one finger extended.

Their forefingers.

Not what you were thinking.

Shame on you.

Robert Florey was an elderly gentleman who'd been directing since the '30s who had gotten his start working with director James Whales, who helmed the original *Frankenstein* in 1931. Paul Stewart was an actor who made his mark playing a squinty-eyed bad guy. You'd know him if you saw him and are over fifty. I got along with Florey, not so well with Stewart. He once told me that whenever I wanted to look angry, all I had to do was squint. It went downhill from there. He did help me pick out the wardrobe for my character. Terrific stuff. Dress jackets, nice slacks, the works. I was cocky and didn't think he knew how to direct and said so. Not the best way to ingratiate yourself with someone who is holding your career in his hands. Especially someone who'd been in the business for forty years. The show lasted two years; I lasted one. Ah, well. Live and learn. If only I *had* learned. My mouth was destined to get me into more trouble down the road.

In *Shayne*, I played the part of college kid, Dick Hamilton, brother to Lucy Hamilton, Michael Shayne's secretary and girl Friday. Patricia Donahue played Lucy, Richard Denning played Shayne. Great people to work with. Dick was the kind of kid that got into everything—sometimes good, sometimes not. I'd either save the day or completely screw it up.

I lived about fifteen minutes from the studio—by car. The problem was that I had lost my license for six months. Speeding. No recourse. So, I rode a bike. Not too bad. Good exercise, and I had a shower in my dressing room, which was at street level, which saved me the trouble of lugging my bike up the rickety wooden stairs.

However . . . there was a Western shooting on the lot at the same time: *Wanted, Dead or Alive* (1958), starring Steve McQueen, who had a very nice second-floor dressing room. He didn't care for it. He would rather have a first-floor dressing room. He mentioned to the studio head that "Gary's would be perfect." And he got it. I argued and got nowhere. I talked to McQueen. He said "No." I called him something scatological and told him he'd never make it in the business. Wonder if that's why I never worked with him.

I had gone through a few agents by this time. I found Ronnie Leif while I was working on *Shayne* and we hit it off right away. Finding Ronnie was the break of my career. He was married to Lew Wasserman's daughter. That may not mean much to you, but Lew Wasserman was the head of The Music Corporation of America (MCA) and the head honcho at Universal Studios. My agent was married to *his* daughter! The implications, the possibilities were enormous.

I knew Ronnie could open doors. It was up to me what I did when I got in.

Christmas Card

I believe this is called a *non sequitur*. It is simply that I thought of it very late one night while sitting at the computer and thought you might get a chuckle out of it.

For several years, right around *The Virginian* era, I used to make my Christmas Cards. Funny but not blasphemous. This one was my favorite. Left picture was on the front, right was on the inside, like usual. Merry Christmas, every one.

Tis Tyme to Light the Lights of Yule

Gary's Christmas Card. c. 1961.

NINETEEN – Universal Studios

I auditioned but I don't remember anything about it. In fact, I may not have auditioned at all. If I remember correctly, they saw a few segments of *Michael Shayne*, liked what they saw, and put me under a seven-year contract. What that meant was that they would pay me so much per week for forty weeks a year for seven years. That gave them the right to use me in any of the Universal shows that were shooting at the time. *Wagon Train, Laramie, Alfred Hitchcock Presents, Thriller* with Boris Karloff, *Bachelor Father* (where I gave Noreen Corcoran her first screen kiss), *Laredo, Rawhide, Tales of Wells Fargo* (all circa 1960), and many, many more. I got to do most of them. An actor's dream. And on top of everything, I got my very own street-level dressing room. I sent McQueen a "Poop on You" card, which, I might add, he never answered.

The studio worked me a lot and I was lovin' it. Different parts. Different actors. Different directors. Learning-my-craft-on-the-job, as it were. So when screen tests for *The Virginian* (1962) were announced, I felt ready. I got the screen test material and studied/practiced day and night. I even wrote a song that I thought might be appropriate for "Steve Hill" (my character) to sing. Aside from all that, I was able to find out that they wanted Steve's character to be light and a bit comedic but to also have a strong serious side when necessary. "Perfect!"

Testing! Testing!

They said there were about five hundred guys up for the part of "Steve," and I saw most of them. I was positive they were the same guys that auditioned for *Dragstrip Riot*. I didn't care. I was going to give it everything I had. One lucky break for me was that I was to audition with Doug McClure, who wound up with the part of "Trampas." Doug and I had known each other socially and liked each other's sense of humor, so we got together beforehand and worked out a couple of routines we thought might be fun. One gag we did had me facing Doug, then jumping up in the air and straddling him. He caught me with his arms under my legs, throwing them upward, sending me into a back flip off of him. It worked like a charm.

They say all's fair in love and war and auditions, but it can still piss you off. The rules were strict and clear. Unless paired with one or more actors, NO OTHER ACTORS were allowed on the test set, which most all of the actors agreed to and acted accordingly. But there was one actor, Ben "The Pooper" Cooper, who had other ideas.

Ben was one of many who were up for the part of "Steve Hill." He'd been around a while, done several movies, and *really* wanted this part. Ben had a producer friend at Universal, and together they schemed and invaded the testing area and sat around watching all the other "Steve Hill" auditionees and commenting in not very subtle ways. "Tacky! Tacky! Tacky!" But we all held our own. At one point, Doug approached them and reminded them that it was a closed set. They apologized profusely and said they were just leaving. They never did.

The final part of the test was to have about ten or fifteen of the actors auditioning for "Steve" or "Trampas" all gather in front of the camera and do whatever we wanted. Doug and I couldn't have asked for anything better. We ran rampant. Flips, jokes, burlesque bits, whatever. My favorite part was when Doug found a feather boa used by one of the saloon girls and, unbeknownst to Ben, hooked it onto his butt, which he wore for almost the entire audition piece. The look on his face when he finally discovered his "boa tail" was priceless. Oh, he was livid. He actually demanded to do the whole test scene over again. The director, laughing, said no. The cameraman, laughing, said no. All of the actors, roaring and lifting Doug onto their shoulders, said no. Even Ben's producer friend was laughing. Doug had the final word: "Ben. You never looked better."

Now it was time for the waiting game. The powers that be (or were) had to look at all the tests, make sure the chemistry between the actors worked, all the stuff that they do to put a show like this together. So we waited.

Jerre Hinshaw, a big wig at Universal, was always a champion for me. Always encouraging, always a listener. And if I was out of line, he was never too bashful to tell me so. We should all have friends like Jerre. After the tests, I asked if he could give me a hint as to who got the part of Steve.

"Gary," he said. "I could give you a hint. But if I did then I'd have to give the part to Ben Cooper."

I stopped asking. A day or so later, I was invited to a party at Jerre's home. Don't remember what the occasion was. What I do remember is arriving at Jerre's home and ringing the doorbell. Jerre answered the door and I would have sworn that the first words he uttered were:

"Oh, hi, Steve."

"What?! What did you say?"

Jerre, with wide-eyed innocence, responded. "What? You mean just now when I said 'Hi'?"

"I heard the 'hi!' I mean after that! What did you call me?"

"Gary," he placated. "You're hearing things. Relax. Come on. I'll introduce you around."

Which he did. It was a terrific party, but my mind kept harking back to what I was sure Jerre said at the door. But he was mute, silent, and was in complete denial of having said anything of the sort. The party was a huge success and everybody had a great, great time. Including me. But . . . I was still going nuts!

The next day my agent called and said that I was to play the part of "Steve" on *The Virginian*. I had actually gotten the part. All the work had paid off. I'm sure that working and testing with Doug played a major role in the studio's decision to cast me. What a blessing! Thanks, Doug. *The Virginian* was the first 90-minute Western television series ever. And, it was sold without a pilot.

TWENTY – And We're Off

Lee J. Cobb, James Drury, Doug McClure, Roberta Shore, Pippa Scott and yours truly were the first to be cast as "regulars" on our show. Scripts had to be written, sets built, publicity photos and stories generated and distributed, radio, TV, and public appearances scheduled. Wardrobe fitted, dressing rooms assigned, and our own personal horses chosen.

Speaking of horses. I forgot to mention that during the screen testing interviews, one of the questions they had asked me was a simple one:

"Can you ride a horse?" And I gave them a simple answer: "Yes."

It wasn't true, but it was simple. I'd never been on a horse before in my life—unless you want to count that pony ride I took, strapped to the saddle, with my mom leading me around in a circle. I was six.

First cast of
The Virginian c. 1962

Babe

I'd considered myself fairly athletic and figured that I had time to learn the basic fundamentals of horsebacking. We had a month or two between the time we were cast and shooting started. Plenty of time.

Not an immediate priority. Then, before I knew it, we were ready to shoot the first show of this new, history-making Western on the next Monday. I was sitting around on the Friday before the aforementioned Monday thinking, *Maybe this weekend.* But it never happened. The first five days of shooting were the interior scenes, the last five would be the exteriors, you know, the wide open plains, campfires and beans, cattle grazing, rustlers rustling. I still had plenty of time. Nay, nay, dear reader!

The setup for the *first* shot of the *first* day of the *first* show was this: Fifty horses, gathered and ready to go. A very long fence (half mile) running along a stretch of flat, open prairie. A camera car on a dirt road on one side of the fence, and Jim, Doug, or me and the horses on the other. The shot: The horses are running full out. The camera car right alongside shooting over and through them at *The Virginian* riding hell-bent in and around those huffing, snorting, thundering equines, herding them, maneuvering them, keeping them in a group. Then, after the horses, Drury and the camera car had traveled the length of the fence, the horses were stopped, rounded up and returned to their starting position.

Four people on the show knew I'd never been on a horse: Jim, Doug, Gary Combs, my stunt double, and Gary's dad, Del Combs, who was the head wrangler. Jim had worked years on a dude ranch and owned horses. Doug had rodeoed for years. They were fine. They knew what they were doing. Me, I needed help. So I turned to Gary and his dad. They laughed as I explained my predicament. I said I failed to see the humor in the situation. They stopped laughing. Probably because they'd noticed I had peed my pants.

I'd been practicing mounts all morning, so I told them that I could probably get on the horse, and maybe even manage to *stay* on for the whole shot. My main concern was stopping. What if I lose control? What if my horse realizes that I'd never been on a horse

Babe and Gary in a scene from *The Virginian* c. 1962

before and decides to have some fun at my expense? What if he or she takes off, unfettered by the person on his or her back, and winds up in south central L.A.? Riderless? What if they never find where I had been tossed or thrown or whatever they call it and I lie there for weeks, maggots covering my body, stuffing themselves? (I had a vivid imagination.)

Gary and Del smirked. "Not a problem," they said encouragingly. "We've got the perfect horse for you." And they trotted out this *big* bay mare with a white spot on her forehead. "Babe," said Del. "Meet Gary." She looked at me and laughed. She actually laughed.

That wouldn't have been so bad, but she rolled around on her back, holding her stomach, tongue lolling out. And every time she looked my way she laughed harder. It was very disconcerting. Then, suddenly, she stopped, got up, looked me in the eye and said, *Just kidding*. Then licked my face in apology.

<u>*NOTE*</u>: *You have to understand that stunt doubles couldn't be used in this particular shot. The whole purpose of the shot was for the camera to zoom in and out on the face of the rider (Jim, Doug or me) to show that we were the real deal. Easy for Jim, with all that dude ranching experience behind him. As for Doug, a piece of cake with his rodeo background. Besides, whatever Doug did he looked great. Who wouldn't with 82 perfect teeth, all in front.*

Jim went first. Then Doug. Flawless. Beautiful. They made it looked effortless. Tom Mix, Roy Rogers and even Ben Johnson would have found other careers had they seen Jim and Doug doing their stuff.

I was on deck and getting last minute pointers from Gary and Del. "At the end of the run just point Babe toward us and we'll have wranglers all lined up ready to stop her. Got it?"

"Piece 'o cake," I replied, not believing a word. The assistant director approached me.

"We're ready for you, Gary. Do you want to ride up to the start point?"

"No!" I blurted. " I'd rather walk." I did. It was a short walk. Not much time for stalling. Then, during that walk to the start point, something changed for me. Don't ask me what but . . . I was committed. I'd come too far to fail now. It was do or die and if I was going to die I was going out in a blaze, by God. "Look out, Babe. Here I come!"

As I said, I'd been practicing mounts. I picked the one I wanted. The one where you grab the reins, jump up, and while you're *in the* air you jam your left foot into the stirrup and swing your right leg over the horse and sit. The only problem with this particular mount is that if I missed, I could find myself flat on my ass, or . . . if I got my foot caught, Babe could take off like a bullet and in a short, bouncy, scratchy while, I'd find myself, yes, in South Central L.A. No, dammit! I was committed! I didn't care! No more pussy-footin' around! It's go for broke time! So I tried the mount. Yes, I did and did it perfectly. I surprised the hell out of myself.

Ironically, the director happened to be looking my way at the time. He grinned, waved and gave me a thumbs-up. Oh, little did he know.

The moment had come. The horses were in place, the wranglers were ready to whip them up and the camera car was in position with engines revving. Time stopped. Nothing moved. It was just Babe and me. Now that she wasn't laughing I ventured forth, leaned over her neck and whispered: "Babe. Listen to me. The pressure's on. But I promise you, if you get me through this you will find your stall filled nightly with apples, carrots and sugar cubes for the rest of your life. Waddya say?" She did that flubbery thing that horses do with their lips, turned, looked at me, winked, and said, *It's in the bag, Gar. And I'll hold you to your promise. As for the apples, I prefer Granny Smiths.*

The camera rolled. The director said "Action!" The wranglers stampeded the horses. I jabbed Babe with my spurs, and we were off! In half a second, she was at full speed and running smooth as glass. She'd done it. *We'd* done it! Babe and I were one! We were weaving in and out of those wild (apparently) horses like there was no tomorrow. I was whipping my reins around, swinging my hat, whooping and hollering. At one point when we were stuck behind a slow moving stallion, I would swear that I heard Babe yell, *Move it, lard ass!* Whether she did or not doesn't matter, the stallion moved.

At one moment we were on the far side of the herd and the next we were five feet from the camera car. "Easy, Babe," I said. "Not too close to the camera!" *Stifle it,* she replied. *This is your close up!* From that point on I never argued with Babe.

The shot was over and it was time to stop. Now, what was it I was supposed to . . . Oh, yeah. Aim Babe toward Gary, Del, and the guys. I did. But as I approached them, Babe did the strangest thing. She'd start to stop—abruptly—then she'd go again, just as abruptly. Stop! Start! Stop! Start! She kept it up until Gary grabbed her bridle and brought her to a stop. That's when I bailed off of Babe's back. I was about to drop to my knees and kiss her hooves when the director ran up, Jim and Doug right behind him.

"Gary!" he wailed. "That was sensational! Brilliant! Superb! I've never seen anything so . . . so . . . Well, I haven't. It was classic! Jim! Doug! Why couldn't you have done it like Gary?!?" Then he kissed me on the lips and pranced off. Jim and Doug each gave me "one of those looks" that said, *You haven't heard the last of this, fella!* And they walked off, conspiratorially designing something dastardly involving me.

There was still the issue of Babe's "stop/start" routine. I asked Gary and Dell what had happened. They were laughing. Everybody was always laughing, and I was getting a complex. They finally managed to stop long enough to tell me that part of what I had done to stop Babe was right. Like pulling back on the reins. That's what you do to make a horse stop. What I shouldn't have done was grab her with my legs so that my spurs jabbed at her sides. It's referred to as "mixed signals." Babe was doing her best to do what I was signaling, it was just that I had no idea in hell what I was signaling. I turned to Babe, scratched her jowls, and apologized profusely. She nuzzled my cheek and said, *S'alright, kid. You and me are gonna be fine. Get on. We got some work to do.*

Babe and I were inseparable for the rest of the day. I rode her everywhere. Up steep hills. Down steep hills. Racing along dusty roads. Up to her waist in a small lake. Through the woods to grandma's house. We didn't even stop for lunch. If Babe had been able to cook, I'd'a married her. We lost all track of time. So much so that when it was time for our next shot, they had to send riders out to find us.

It was a simple shot, especially now that I was an expert horseman. Jim, Doug, and I were to ride down this road at a slow gallop, pass in front of the camera, which would then pan with us and photograph our backs as we cantered into the sunset. I was positioned on the outside, which put me closest to the camera as we rode by. Like I said, simple. I was so caught up in my new-found equinistic abilities that I failed to notice "that expression" on Jim and Doug's faces. In retrospect, I think it said something like *Your ass is grass, Jack.* I also should have sus-
pected something when they
insisted that I ride on the outside—closest to the edge of the
road.

"Action!" We're off at a
good clip heading down the
road. All was well as we passed
the camera. It was then I began
to notice that my part of the
road was getting narrower. In
fact, disappearing completely.
I was riding in the briars and

Publicity w/ Jim, Doug,
Barbara Luna and me.

brambles and heading for a five-foot bush! Somewhere from under me I heard someone say, *A little faith, please.* With that, Babe leaped into the air and I, instinctively, leaned forward. She cleared the bush with a foot to spare and I, instinctively, sat upright. She began her descent and I, instinctively, leaned backwards. She landed lighter that a butterfly on a leaf as if it had been a move she made every day and twice on Sunday. Jim and Doug were stupefied. The director was orgasmic. "Gary! That was sensational! Outstanding! You are a director's dream come true! Jim! Doug! Why couldn't you guys do it like that?" He walked off and Jim and Doug beat the snot out of their horses. As I pointed out to them shortly thereafter: "When you got it, you got it."

One, two, three…Nope. That ain't it either.

TWENTY ONE –
Connie, Me and . . . Her!!

By now Connie was knocking 'em dead at Warner Bros. A hit series, *Hawaiian Eye* (1959), a big movie with Jerry Lewis, *Rockabye Baby* (1958), recording contracts, guest spots, and all that goes with a burgeoning career. We'd planned on getting married, twice, and for one reason or another, called them off. Reasons are irrelevant.

We'd been to the Academy Awards twice before as guests of Warner Bros. This time, Universal was picking up the tab. This year's event was taking place in Santa Monica, CA. in a huge auditorium, and as usual the event was star-studded, glitzy, dazzling, and toothy. I don't remember who won what because what happened as we were leaving the auditorium eclipsed all that had occurred earlier that evening.

Her

All the celebs and VIP's had had their cars taken and parked by elaborately-trained valets and, following the event, said valets would return all cars to their rightful owners or renters. The celebs (Connie and I were now considered "celebs") had a special exit to facilitate and expedite the retrieving of our cars: Out of the auditorium, through two large double doors, and onto a ramp stretching from the inside first floor, down to the outside street level. It was a fairly long ramp, about twenty feet wide and sixty feet long. It slanted so that the people in front were below you and the people behind were above you (*This* is an important element of the story). People where chatting and laughing. The mood was light and fun. Every minute or so, we hear an appropriate-sounding voice from some discretely hidden loud speaker announce: "Miss Katherine Hepburn's car." "Mr. Cary Grant's car." I was excited. In a few minutes, they were going to announce "Mr. Gary Clarke's car" in front of all of these stars. But the best was yet to come.

As Connie and I stood there, watching our various heroes and heroines getting into their cars, I thought I heard someone behind me call my name. I turned abruptly and found (O, thank you, Lord) my nose about 3/4 of an inch from the most incredibly-beautiful cleavage I had ever seen. It breathed and swelled, decreasing the distance to my nose to 1/4 of an inch. Slowly, my eyes moved upward. The swan-like neck. The perfect chin. Full and beckoning lips. The dark, almond-shaped eyes. The raven-black hair. Her sweet breath enveloping my nose. I was face-to-face, I mean *really* face-to-face, with Sofia Loren. I may have experienced an orgasm, I'm not sure. I was transfixed, and she didn't retreat a centimeter. She just stood there, smiling down at me.

It was a good thing that I had had the training and experience I'd had. Being a star myself, I knew how to handle myself in a clinch. I knew how to deal with those little unexpected moments. Cool was my middle name. An opportunity had presented itself and I rose to the occasion. I spoke: "Hababeduh grok myuomg fredunk . . . . " It sounded fine to me at the time.

Somewhere in the far distance I heard people laughing. (Would they never stop?) Then I felt a strange presence. Someone was looking at me. Not in anger, but in benevolence. I looked to Sophia's immediate right and saw him. Carlo Ponti. Sophia's husband. I must have looked completely lost and helpless because he regarded

And *what a her!!*

me with great compassion and, in his deeply resonant Italian voice, consoled me with, "I know."

With that, I looked back into that incredible face and, as if in a dream, she cupped my cheeks with her two hands and planted a big, soft, juicy kiss on my eagerly awaiting lips. People applauded. I'd just been smooched by Sofia Loren! I'm not saying I was affected by the kiss, but I remember nothing about the valet bringing up my car and calling my name. In fact, it wasn't till the next day that I realized I'd left Connie at the auditorium. She was pissed. I didn't care.

It was just a matter of time until Connie and I realized that "we" weren't in the cards. Friends, yes. Spouses, no. We parted amicably and are still good friends and talk often.

Sometime during the late '60s, she called and told me to watch the *Mike Douglas Show* (1961). She was on it. Of course I watched. She and two other female stars were being interviewed about "their first lovers." Well, she spilled the beans. It had happened one afternoon in Byron's Hotel and Rooming House, and she had no qualms discussing it. And it was tasteful and very complimentary. Some techniques were discussed but nothing graphic. It was a bit of a landmark show for its time, and I liked it. I remembering wondering what the fallout might be, and I didn't have to wonder long. I started getting calls from girls/women I hadn't heard from in years and from guys offering their assistance if I was unable to handle the tidal wave.

My date card was filled for months. Thank you, Concetta.

TWENTY TWO –
The First Season

The cast was great. The crew was terrific. The executives were completely supportive. And the scripts were all first class. Good stories with a good moral. And my dressing room was on the first floor. Publicity was pretty good, too. However, there was one incident during the first episode.

We were on the back lot where they had meticulously duplicated the town of Medicine Bow, Wyoming, circa 1890. Gary Combs and I were shooting the breeze as we sat inconspicuously on the "hotel" steps. Extras and a few visitors were scattered about the porch, passing the time and watching the shooting of various scenes. As the events unfolded, I overheard two local reporters in conversation just behind me. One of them was slamming the show already.

"Just what we need," he was saying. "Another stupid Western with stupid scripts and stupid actors. Damn. When is this studio going to wise up? I'll give this turkey half a season."

The guy had no idea I was sitting there. I was pissed off and halfway to my feet when Gary grabbed me and said: "Careful. You're too new. Let Jim or the director handle this." I heeded his warning and went to find Jim. Doug saw me, and I guess my expression prompted him to ask me what was wrong. I told him, and before I could finish he was storming over to the hotel porch. He was on that guy like a blanket. Didn't hit him, but with Doug's nose just inches from his, he knew that he was staring death in the face. He tried to weasel out. "I didn't say that. Who said I said that? I never said any such thing. It a lie! Who said that??" I moved in a bit closer. "I did," I said. "My name's Gary Clarke. I'm a regular on this show, and are you calling me a liar?" I must have been ready to throw a punch because Doug stepped between me and him and Gary grabbed my arm. Punching a reporter would have been the dumbest move of my fledging career. But sometimes . . . y'know . . . you just gotta do dumb things. Thanks to Doug and Gary Combs, I didn't. Oh, yeah, we never saw the reporter again.

Great is Great

I loved Lee J. Cobb. Brilliant actor. Completely professional. And always gave his all in any scene he was in, whether he was on camera or off camera reading lines for his fellow actors.

I remember watching a scene between him and Roberta Shore who played "Betsy," his daughter. Betsy was sick in bed and "daddy" was sitting beside her. They were talking. I watched this scene for four hours. Judge Garth just talking to Betsy in a way that was mesmerizing. It was simple yet so powerful and poignant you couldn't take your eyes off him. Was I in awe? You bet.

It was this awe that began to present a kind of problem for me. I found that when I was around Lee—off camera—I couldn't say two words without tripping over my tongue. Kind of like it was with Sofia. Maybe worse. Jim and Doug could laugh and joke with him, talk about the weather, politics, or whatever, but me . . . I turned into a babbling blob of jello.

After a couple of months, I decided I had to do something about it and I figured the best approach would be head-on. We were scheduled to drive out to location the following day. Jim, Doug, Lee, and I would ride out in the customary limo. I told Jim and Doug what

I was going to do, and they were all for it and would do anything they could to support it.

Jim and the driver were in the front seat. Lee was in the back on the right, Doug in the middle, and I was on the left. We arrived at the location, and Jim, Doug, and the driver got out. It was Lee and me, there, alone, in the back seat. A long, pregnant silence. Lee took out one of his ever-present cigars, lit up and sat back with nary a glance in my direction. I girded myself and spoke up.

Don't believe her! She loved it! Roberta Shore and Gary between scenes on *The Virginian* c. 1962

"Lee," I began. "I want you to know what an honor it is to be working with you. What an incredible opportunity to learn from a master. For a while now, I've noticed that when we're not on camera, you know, just waiting around for the next scene, just kinda . . . hanging out . . . . "

I was feeling stupider and stupider by the second. Get to the damned point, already! "Well, what I've noticed is that I find it almost impossible to carry on any kind of meaningful conversation with you. I'm always tongue-tied with awe. The work you've done. The awards you've won. What could I possibly have to say that would be of any interest to you? We're going to be working together for some time, and I would hate to have me be a complete boob whenever the opportunity arises for you and I to have a conversation. I'm sure you've run into this before, so I was wondering if you might have any suggestions of ways I might get by this awe thing. You know, just be able to speak to you intelligently. Has it happened to you before? Is

Lee J. Cobb on the set of
The Virginian c. 1962

there anything you might tell me that would help?"

I was drenched in sweat. I had at least gotten it out, discombobulated as it was. But I knew it was coming. A pearl of wisdom that would change my life forever. A gem that would be inscribed in *The Book of Life*. I looked at him, waiting for it. Long silence. He drew deeply on his cigar and let the smoke curl out easily into the confines of that back seat. Any moment now. But nothing came. For minutes that seemed like hours. Was he mulling it over? Did he want to make sure he gave me the perfect response? Did he have a hearing problem? I waited as long as I thought prudent. I spoke again.

"I realize," I resumed, noticing a new determination in my voice. "I realize that this is probably not a huge priority for you, and it wasn't my intention to intrude into your space, but I had to do something and I thought speaking to you would be the thing to do. If I've offended you in any way, I apologize. But if there is anything you can tell me that would help, it would be greatly appreciated. Is there *anything* at all that you think might help?"

Still no look in my direction. Another puff. Another exhalation. And another eternity of time passing. Not a word. Not a grunt. Not a hint that I even existed in his consciousness. I had spilled my guts and this is what I get?!? Yes, I was a tad upset.

"Well excuse me all to hell!" I shot at him. "Excuse me for

intruding on your precious time! As far as I'm concerned you can kiss my ass and you know where you can stick that cigar!!" I was out of the car and storming my way to my dressing room. I passed Jim and Doug, who were grabbing their breakfast at the chuck wagon.

"How'd it go," they asked.

"I told him to kiss my ass!" I spat out.

"Oh, good," said Jim. "We thought maybe it wasn't going well."

Now the irony of the whole thing is that most of my scenes that day were with Lee. Did I care? Not a whit. When we were in a scene together I gave it everything I had. When we were not shooting, he didn't exist. After several scenes with Lee, the director came up to me.

"Gary. I don't know what's going on, but keep it up. These scenes are great!"

So it went throughout the day. Lee and I "tore up the scenery." I didn't care; he was Lee, and that's the way it was. I didn't give it a second thought. Then, the final scene of the day, which was, of course, with Lee and me. Lee was sitting in his director's chair (we all had one), smoking another one of those damned cigars. I was pacing back and forth, ready and anxious to get into the scene. The last one I'd have to do with this selfish, self-centered, compassionless human being. I don't know why, but I inadvertently glanced in his direction. He was looking at me and there was this mischievous glint in his eye. It hit me like a Mack truck. I walked up to him. Looked at him for a long moment.

"You son-of-a . . . You did all that on purpose!! What a

Director Earl Bellamy,
Jack Klugman and GC in
"Roar From the Mountain"

rotten . . . ." He burst into that famous Lee J. Cobb laugh, stood up and grabbed me in the best bear hug I've ever had." From that day until the day he died we were fast friends. He truly did turn my life around. To think that a man like that would take the time with a punk like me, well . . . no one is too big or too small for our love and compassion. God bless you, Lee.

I would guess that it was because of Lee J. Cobb that our show was able to attract the big name stars that it did. Bette Davis. Robert Redford. George C. Scott. Lee Marvin. Charles Bronson.

One of my favorites was Ricardo Montalban. What a sweet, joyous man he was. Loved his wife and family and was constantly talking about them. When you talked to him, he listened, generously and with interest. His true perspective in life showed itself one day

Our animals were always well trained.

when we were on location. It was a hot, dusty day, the air conditioners in our dressing rooms weren't working and the insects were running rampant. All in all, a miserable day.

Doug, Ricky, and I were standing in line for lunch, making our way along the tables laid out with a variety of food. Usually it was pretty good, but on this day, on this 130-in-the-shade day, nothing was any good. Doug and I were grousing about something, everything, when we noticed that Ricky was smiling and singing, kind of out loud, to himself.

"Ay, Jalisco, Jalisco, Jalisco, tu tienes tu novia que es Guadalajara..."

Doug and I thought the sun was getting to him.

"Ricky," we said. "It's 180 degrees out here. It's dusty, even the flies won't eat the food, and you're singing some jaunty, jolly Mexican song. Are you nuts?"

He looked at us with that great smile of his, grabbed us each around the neck, pulled us close and said, "Oh, my friends. Where else can you work in the great outdoors, doing what you love, have all the food you want, with incredible friends around you? Is this not a wonderful life?"

Try arguing with *that* logic.

Pete, me and two hounds that have to pee, crammed into the back of a
Nash Rambler, and the old man's loving every minute of it.

TWENTY THREE – Digression

That's My Old Man

Time to talk a bit about my dad: Clarke Franklin L'Amoreaux. A big guy. Handsome. 6' 3" and drank like a fish. Intolerant and bigoted. Said he hated "fairies," Jews, and short guys. Ironic, because his best friend for twenty years was Norm Fink, a 5' 5" Jew. Go figure. But, two out of three ain't bad.

Pop had spent several years in the Shore Patrol and was always bragging about the Marines he'd beaten up and the "broads" he'd had. He worked at the May Co. department store for most of his life, starting out as a window trimmer and ending up as manager for all the departments having anything to do with men's clothing and accessories. A big wheel. My brother, Pete, and I are his sons. Pop (he preferred that to "Dad") was what you might call a "man's man." Not unlike the Private Eye movie characters of the late '30s and '40s. He wanted his sons to be "men," and was always testing us for our masculine handshakes. He liked the "real men" like John Wayne, Clark Gable, Lee Marvin, and Rock Hudson, and suggested often that we emulate them.

The day he found out that Rock was gay was a black day for Pop. "Rock Hudson a fairy?! How could I have not seen that. I can spot 'em a mile away. Maybe it's a mistake."

This revelatory discovery of my dad's was nevertheless an extraordinary opportunity for Pete and me. We'd teased him before, but this unexpected event opened up brand new territories for us. We wasted no time. It was easy getting him into a conversation about Rock, and now that I was becoming firmly ensconced in the motion picture and TV industries, I would, of course, have first hand knowledge about such matters.

"Yeah, Pop. I've known about Rock for a long time. I'm surprised you didn't catch it. You're so good at that." He agreed.

"So," I continued, "you probably spotted John Wayne and Clarke Gable right away."

His eyes widened and his jaw dropped. "John Wa . . . Clarke Gab . . . are you saying that they're. . . . "

"Flaming," Pete said.

"He's right, Pop," I confirmed, then elaborated. "I can't believe that you didn't know about them. Everyone knows. John Wayne and Wallace Beery have be an item for years. And MGM had a hell of a time keeping it out of the papers when they found Clarke Gable floating on top of Oliver Hardy in Gable's very own swimming pool. One of the cinematographers on *The Virginian* showed me the photograph."

Pop was crushed. Despite the rough, tough exterior, he was a gullible marshmallow of the first rank and believed all the stories Pete and I made up about some of his other favorites.

Every Christmas Eve for years, Pete and I would drive out to his home in West Covina, California, pick him up, go buy a tree, bring it back to his home, and decorate it. By now, Pop had remarried, Alice was her name, and had a daughter, Kathleen, my half-sister. We'd eat, tell stories, kid Pop, and trim the tree.

One year, Pete and I decided to bring the tree with us. We bought a nice one, tied it to the roof rack on Pete's station wagon, and made our way to Pop's house thinking of a way we might surprise him. In the house, we told him that Pete had bought a new car (he hadn't) and bet Pop that he couldn't guess what it was by just sitting in the front seat. He scoffed and said it'd be a snap. So we blindfolded him, took him out to the car, put him in the front seat with me next to him and Pete behind the wheel (Pete's car had no console). We figured he'd see it was Pete's old car, get out, see the tree and say, "Oh, you guys!" But he didn't. He knew it was Pete's car and figured as long as we were in it we should go buy a tree. Ah-hah! Another opportunity.

Pete's and my mind worked in concert. We knew immediately what we'd do: drive to the tree lot, right behind the May Co. where Pop worked. Pop would get out of the car, see the tree and say, "Oh, you guys!"

It's dark. About 8:30. We pull into this huge parking lot, and the tree lot at the far, far end has maybe six cars parked by its fence. Pete parks a hundred yards from the lot, ninety yards from anything that even resembles another car. Pete says he doesn't want to take the chance of having anyone scratch his paint. Pop buys it, gets out of the car, and heads for the lot. He didn't see the tree. We called but he never turned around. He just waved for us to follow him and kept walking. More possibilities were emerging.

Now we're in the tree lot, and through the fence, about a hundred yards away, bathed in the parking lot lights, was Pete's car with the tree, in all of its pristine beauty, fastened to its top. Pop has spotted the tree he wants. He asks the salesman how much it is. It's $25.

"What?! Twenty-five bucks? For that anemic

Mom and Pop in one of their happier moments. Of course they were divorced at the time.

looking weed? I'll give you five bucks for it."

The bartering began. Pop was good, but he'd met his match. The salesman's position was that if the tree was as bad as Pop says it is, why buy it at any price? Pop's counter was that he needed something for the patio, and besides, if the salesman didn't sell it tonight, he'd only have to burn it the next day. They were at it for forty-five minutes, and Pop had managed to wheedle him down to $7. It was then that I went up to him and, with a sense of forced urgency, said that we had to go. Now! He balked, saying that he had the guy right where he wanted him. I then, very subtly, pointed out that Pete had not only stolen a beautiful tree from this very lot, but had already tied it to the roof of his station wagon. I pointed to said tree tied to the top of said station wagon. Pop blanched. White as a snowball. Fear wracked his body. He turned to the sales guy:

"Ah . . . it's still too . . . ah . . . much. I gotta go . . . it's getting . . . I'll come back . . . tomorrow. I live in . . . ah . . . San Diego!"

He drags me out of the tree lot. "If anyone from the store . . . if they . . . a stolen tree . . . I can't . . . pick me up on the other side of the building." And he was gone. Pete and I picked him up and all he could say till we got back to the house was "Don't tell Alice! Don't tell Alice. Don't tell Kathleen, either. Oh, don't tell Alice." But of course we told Alice—the real story—and she loved it. So did Kathleen.

TWENTY FOUR –
Back On Track

Lee Marvin

This should tie it all together. One of Pop's all-time favorites was Lee Marvin. Macho. Virile. An ex-Marine. Pop's kinda guy. Well, Lee was the guest on one of our shows called "It Tolls For Thee." Talk about bigger than life, that was Lee Marvin. Pretty much the way you see him on the screen was the way he was. Funny. Crass when he wanted to be. A gentleman when he chose that. Professional. Tough.

I wanted to surprise my old man, so I called him and made up a story to get him to the studio. "I think I can make it." That meant he was dying to come. I knew he'd be there.

Lee said he'd be glad to spend a while with my dad swapping war stories and such. This was great. This was really going to be a special day for the old man. I had a limo pick him up at the front gate and bring him to the back lot where we were filming. I met him at the car and walked him over to the set where Lee was waiting by his chair.

"Pop," I said. "This is Mr. Lee Marvin. Lee, this is my dad, Clarke L'Amoreaux."

Lee extended his hand and, surprisingly, Pop was a little slow in taking it. He did, finally, but even I could see what a weak, wimpy handshake it was. What happened to that strong, manly handshake he was always harping on me about? They exchanged a few words then Pop excused himself, saying he had left something in the limo. I apologized to Lee and he made it alright saying that maybe my dad had expected someone else.

Then it hit me. "Oh, good Lord. How could I have forgotten something like that?" I explained to Lee that Pete and I were always spinning yarns and playing tricks on the old man and that one of the yarns we'd spun was that Lee Marvin and Mickey Rooney were a couple.

Lee actually fell down laughing, told me not to worry or say anything to my dad, and that he'd take care of it. By the time lunch time came around, Pop had calmed a bit and was ready to eat where the movie stars eat.

Lunch was catered on the back lot and Pop and I were waiting in line. He was hobnobbing with the elite and loving it. It was about that time Lee walked up and put his arm around Pop's shoulder, their faces very close.

Mickey Rooney publicity photo. c. 1955.

"So, Clarke. Gary tells me that you were in the Shore Patrol. I was in the Marines, y'know. We've probably got a lot in common. Why don't you bring your food into my dressing room? I've got some great bourbon. We can eat, have a few belts, tell stories, you know, get acquainted. Waddya say?"

It was days before Pop would take my phone calls and even longer for him to believe that Lee wasn't gay and had been pulling his chain. He never said he forgave me, but whenever I'd visit him at work, every one of his co-workers I ran in to told me that they'd heard the story.

One of my fondest memories of my old man was the time, following a heated argument about his drinking, that we sat down and talked the whole thing out to completion. At the end, we stood up (an awkward moment) and hugged each other. I told him I loved him and he told me the same. What an extraordinary moment. It was the first time either of us ever did that. I was forty-four.

Tourists

Things moved very smoothly through the first season. At least as far as I knew. The show grew in popularity. Fan mail was picking up. And I still had my dressing room on the ground floor. The Universal Tours were nothing like they are today. What they had then were great big Tanner Line busses that they'd fill (somewhere) with about fifty tourists. They'd drive these behe-

Doug McClure and Gary during a pleasant moment. c. 1963.

moths onto the lot, and if we were shooting on a sound stage, that's where they'd stop.

The wide-eyed tour-takers would be led onto the set, they'd watch some of the machinations that go on while setting up a shot, then they'd watch the actors do their stuff. Sometimes it was an intrusion, but mostly it was fine. And we'd had orders from the front office to "be nice" to the tourists. After all, they'd each paid $10 or

But sometimes you just had to let 'em know!

$20 to come see us.

They did the same thing when we were on the back lot. Busses would show up, people would get out, stand where they wouldn't interfere with the shot, and snap their Kodaks till their little fingers were sated. There were, from time to time, a few faux pas. Example: The Virginian, Trampas, and Steve were in the midst of a shootout with the bad guys right on the main street of Medicine Bow. We were getting the best of them. But Steve was in danger! Will his friends be able to save him?? Would this be the end of Steve? Just as we were about to find out, a Tanner Bus pulled into the middle of the scene and stopped. Oops. "CUT!!!" screamed the director and, as expected, we'd hear the inevitable from the driver: "Sorrrry." At which point, he'd back out of the shot and we do the whole thing all over again. But . . . we were on our *honor* to be nice.

And nice we were. Especially Doug and me. One our favorite "bus-welcoming" routines was this: The bus would arrive, and before anyone could get off, Doug and I would get on, walk up the aisle, looking for the "school teacher from Boise." There was always one. We'd spot her, throw her over our shoulders and carry her off the bus. Usually, she was screaming. Doug and I would disappear with her behind a large rock or bush and make loud and suggestive noises. Moments later, we would emerge looking completely disheveled and worn out. Our "teacher" would emerge, blushing and embarrassed, having loved every minute of it. If we had it on us, Doug and I would hand her a few dollars, regard her with immense awe, and limp away.

Doug McClure and Gary on the set of *The Virginian* c. 1963

Meeting Pat Woodell

My second wife. I didn't know it at the time, but God really has all kinds of ways to surprise us. My friend, Kelly Gordon, a great songwriter and singer (he wrote "That's Life" for Sinatra), told me about this new girl in town who had just been put under contract to Warner Bros. and sang better that Barbara Streisand. She was recording with a huge orchestra, and Kelly invited me to go. He'd written a song for her. I think I wanted to go more just to see what Kelly was all "het up" about than to hear another pretty girl sing a song. Did I say pretty! Oh! Nay, nay, thou great, boorish, inarticulate clump. Not pretty. Stunning and beautifully gorgeous, and I'm being conservative.

I'm sworn to secrecy under penalty of ostracism from anything I may belong to, so I can't/won't give you all the details of our courtship. What I can say is that

Pat Woodell publicity photo. c. 1960.

after the first couple of dates, that was it. I was hooked. Smitten. Rocked back on my heels. And it just got better from there. Pat was working on *Petticoat Junction*, I on *The Virginian*. She was recording and touring with Liberace.

I was recording, too. It's true, I was. Kelly Gordon had written lyrics for the theme from *The Virginian* and I was going to record it for Decca Records. Not because I had the greatest voice. I didn't. But I could carry a tune well enough, and Decca had an orchestra big enough to drown out any "clunkers" I might make.

TWENTY FIVE –
50 Million Viewers

"The Theme From the Virginian" ("Lonesome Tree") did okay. Not a million seller, but it made it into the Top 300 on the charts. Look, I *told* them all I wasn't a singer. The truth is, I'm "meterly challenged." Most of the time, I can't tell if I'm on "a-one-and-a-two" or "a-two-and-a-three." And it does make a difference. Ask any musician. If it's Dixieland, then that's another story. Or even Big Band stuff. With those, I seem to be able to hold my own. When you're in a recording studio, recording a song, you have the opportunity to do it over and over again. I know because that's what I did. Taking two or three hours to record a three-minute song is not unusual. At least in my case it isn't. Then, after they've taken all of the best takes, spliced them together, and smoothed out everything, you have (usually) a decently-recorded song.

What's interesting, though, is despite the fact that I am not a singer (except for singing in choirs or various groups), I managed to record for most of the major labels of the time: RCA Victor, 20th Century Fox, Decca, Capitol, etc. But, if one was to investigate that era and the people who recorded, one would find that a large major-ity of those people should have *never* recorded. Now I know that the rationale behind the push to record me was simply because I was on *The Virginian* and they wanted to see what the traffic would bear. I'd sung solos before. Las Vegas, Lake Tahoe and even a few venues in L.A. But that's different. You're on stage, the music is rockin', your adrenaline is pumping, and you sing. The energy is different. You move, you sell it, you dazzle 'em with your footwork, and you make it. Behind a mic, in a recording studio, all you've got is your voice, if you've got a voice, but whatever you've got, that's what people hear.

"Tonight's The Night"

Let me give you an idea of what can happen. Toward the end of *The Virginian*'s first season, *Photoplay Magazine* voted me "The Most Promising Actor of 1962/1963," an award I was to receive on *The Tonight Show with Johnny Carson (1962)*. Marilyn Monroe had received the award the year before. No relevance, just a point of interest. For me, a big deal.

The whole cast was supportive. Doug said he was going to fly to New York on his own just to hold my hand. Our producers, wanting to take full advantage of the situation, decided that it would be a brilliant idea for me to sing the "Virginian Theme" on the show. "Wouldn't that be better than just sitting there and talking?" They convinced themselves, and it was decided: I was going to sing on The Tonight Show. Piece of cake. Nothing to worry about. Only 50 million TV viewers watching. I told them I'd be fine. I go on, lip sync the song, then sit down and chat with Johnny. What could go wrong?

"Lip sync? Who said anything about lip sync? You're going to sing live! With Skitch Henderson and the Tonight Show orchestra. Great musicians, every one. Should anything go wrong, and we're sure it won't, Skitch and the guys will cover for you." I didn't like it. But they were right. It was a great orchestra, and I was sure they wouldn't let me look like a fool. I arrived at the studio, schlepping a good-sized carry-on filled with all the sheet music from my original recording session. The orchestra was in place, and they were rehearsing with Della Reese, a sensational singer. She was doing two songs that night, and she went over them until she was absolutely sure they were just the way she wanted them. "Yes, Miss Reese. No, Miss Reese. As many times as you like, Miss Reese. We're here for you, Miss Reese," said Skitch.

Two hours! She was wonderful, but still . . . two hours?!? She finished and the band applauded. So did I. When she was gone, Skitch flicked a look my way and asked, "You the TV Western kid?"

"I'm Gary Clarke, Mr. Henderson. I'm going to receive. . . . "

"Got your music?" he asked in a not-too-friendly way. I handed him the music and he proceeded to hand/toss the various parts out to the musicians. I offered. "This is the first time I've done anything like. . . . "

"Okay, guys," he barked at the musicians. "Rock and roll beat. One, two, one, two, three . . . . " And they were off. I jumped in somewhere along the line, recognizing a piece of a musical phrase from time to time. Before I knew, it they were finished. "Okay," says Skitch. "That's it. Be back at five." And they were gone. "Ah, Mr. Henderson, I'm . . . not sure that . . . . "

"Don't worry, kid. We do this all the time. You'll be fine." And he was gone.

Me, Suzanne Pleshette, Bette Davis, Richard Chaimberlain
Award winners on *The Tonight Show* c. 1963

Showtime. Johnny's monologue. Suzanne Pleshette receives her award for "Most Promising Actress." Then Johnny introduces me. The music starts as a stage hand pulls the curtain back and I enter and take my place center stage. The music sounds vaguely familiar. What the hell. I jump in. It seemed like the right place. I sang, the orchestra played. Through the song we went. And the orchestra, Skitch and all his musicians, finished fifteen seconds before I did.

I was on stage, on The Tonight Show, singing, in front of 50 million people, with no band! A dropped pin would have been louder than the applause. I walked, as I had been directed, over to the guest chair next to Johnny's desk (a very long walk). Johnny had that little mischievous grin that he used to get, and he was doing

that drumming-the-pencil-on-the-desk thing that he did. I have to say that there was never a talk show host like this man. Absolutely brilliant. He knew those special "moments" when they'd show up, and he played them. He must have known that I had something on my mind, so he just waited as we both played the pregnant pause. I broke the silence.

Some play by ear. Some don't.

"Johnny, do you happen to have that award thing I'm getting tonight?"

"Yeah," he went along. "Right here."

He reached down beside his desk, came up with the plaque and handed it to me. I took it and looked it over carefully, front and back, then returned it saying, "Doesn't say anything about singing." Johnny laughed, the audience laughed and evaporated some of the "ohness." At least they knew that I knew.

About two weeks later I got a piece of fan mail from a very pretty twenty-seven year old (she'd enclosed her picture).

"Gary," she wrote. *"Congratulations on your very prestigious award. I watch* The Virginian *all the time and you are my favorite actor. You are a wonderful actor and I love you. Please don't sing anymore."*

Love always.

Louise"

See what I mean?

Not The Lot!

People at the studio ribbed me a little. I remember Bob Fuller (*Laramie*) telling me he'd be glad to dub in his voice for mine any time I was going to appear in front of 50 million people again. I warned him: "Look out, big fella. I don't get mad. I get even."

One of the fan magazines wanted to do a motorcycle layout with me. Problem was I didn't own a bike. So I called Honda, told them who I was and what the fan mag wanted to do. They thought it would be a great idea, mainly because of the publicity. They agreed to leave a brand new bike for me at the plant, one I could use on the street *and* in the dirt. I could keep it as long as I wanted, and all I had to do was go down and pick it up. Which I did.

The magazine layout went beautifully and eventually showed up on bookshelves across the country. I was having such a good time, I was reluctant to return the bike to Honda right away. I rode it everywhere. In the hills, on dates, to the store, out to see my relatives, everywhere. I rode it onto the lot as well. Now, riding your bike onto the Universal lot was permitted as long as you parked it as soon as possible. But there was absolutely *no* riding around the hills in the back lot! But I thought I'd try it anyway, way out in the back lot where "Shiloh Ranch" had been built. No one was shooting in the immediate area. Who'd notice?

After about thirty minutes of tearing around the hills, through and around the ranch and chasing a deer, I heard a siren. I stopped, looked, and saw the ever-present little red jeep that Security used to patrol the property. They had me. The guard pulled up next to me and got out, his little ticket book in hand.

"You do know that you're not supposed to be tearing up the landscape with that motorcycle, don't you?"

"I was just practicing," I said. "Didn't think anyone would care."

"I care," he snapped back. "And just what were you practicing for?"

"A magazine layout. I'm an actor here. I'm starring in a series."

Completely unimpressed, he put me in my place. "Well, Mr. Actor. Nobody rides motorcycles on this lot. You're going on report. And if I see you riding that bike anywhere but off the lot, I'll have you arrested. What's your name?"

"You don't know me?"

"If I knew you I wouldn't be asking you name, now, would I?"

"Bob Fuller," I responded. "I'm the star of Laramie. Everyone knows me."

"Well, Mr. Fuller, I don't. And you're still going on report. And remember what I said about the bike. Off the lot. Now!"

I graciously complied.

A few days later, Jim, Doug, and I were having lunch in the commissary. I'd just told them about the incident when Bob walked up.

"The damnedest thing just happened," he said. "Security just reamed my ass for riding a motorcycle on the back lot. They had me in there for an hour. I thought they were gonna ride me off the lot on a rail."

Doug said, "Bobby. Don't ever ride your bike on the back lot."

Jim said, "Yeah. It's against the law."

I said, "I'm booked on *The Tonight Show* again, but I can't ask you to sing for me now that you're a felon."

He left never having the feeling of being heard. Oh, if you see Bob, please don't mention this story. Okay? Knew you'd understand.

One More Pop

I've got to tell one more on my old man. And if he were still here, he'd love it.

My sister, Kathleen, was getting married. A sweet wedding in a Catholic church. Organ music. Choir singing. Nice stuff. Afterwards, the reception was arranged for by my father, who was not known for his extravagance. My dad was strange in that way. He would die for his kids, unless it cost him money. Suffice it to say he was a skinflint. But a lovable one.

He rented a meeting hall. A small meeting hall. One where a small, out-of-the-way group of Masons might congregate. If you had forty people in that hall at the same time, it might be hard to catch your breath. Decorations were a few streamers, a sign screaming "Congratulations," and a paper tablecloth for the cake table. On one end of said table were four bottles of Andre champagne flanked by a dozen or so plastic champagne glasses. At the other end was a large plastic bowl with scalloped edges containing something that looked like pink lemonade. A few chrome bowls of nuts, some small paper plates, and a few plastics forks were scattered about. Muzak provided the music.

Kathleen couldn't have cared less. She and her new husband were hopelessly in love, reception or not. They hardly noticed. Ain't love grand?

That was the reception hall. The personnel roster was a little light, too. One nice waitress to serve the cake and things, and one bartender behind the bar in the corner. A "pay-for-your-own" bar.

Several adults, including Pete and me, attended, but mostly it was Kathleen's friends from school. Pete and I teased Pop into buying two more bottles of champagne and another bowl of peanuts. Alice, Pop's wife, teased him, too, about being a cheapskate, but as long as Kathleen was happy, it didn't matter that the whole reception thing cost him about $150.

These circumstances were prime breeding grounds for one of Pete's and my "Get Pop" things. He hadn't paid the bill yet, so we got the waitress to help us tally up another bill. A "special" bill:

Room:	$250 (not $50)
Champagne:	$32 per bottle (not $7)
Cake:	$202 (not $19)
Peanuts:	$100 (not $15—had to buy the whole box)
Bar Tax:	$175 for excise tax
Security:	$100 Trouble sometimes happens at weddings
Muzak:	$85 (4-hour minimum)
Waitress:	$300
Bartender:	$300
Fire Marshall:	$130
TOTAL:	-----------
	$1674

While we were figuring out the "bill," Pop was schmoozing with the guests, bragging on his daughter and making sure they knew that one of his sons was a TV star. In fact, he was feeling so magnanimous that, after making sure there were only four adults at the bar, he sat with them and boldly announced, "A drink for all these folks. On me!" He was in the middle of his magnanimity when the waitress handed him the "check." He was on his feet.

"What?!? This isn't my . . . Wait! Hold those drinks! Mine, too!"

He raced over to Alice who was privy to the whole thing and waiting for him.

"Did you see this?!" waving the bill in front of her face. She took it and perused it calmly.

"Seems right to me," she said in wide-eyed innocence. Pete and I were pillars of restraint.

"What's the matter, Pop?"

"What's the matter?!? Look at this!" He

"Had I known it was going to cost this much, I would'a kept her!"

shoved the bill at us. We gave it serious consideration.

"Wow, Pop. You're amazing. You really got a great deal," I said.

"No one can get Muzak for less than a 12-hour minimum," Pete offered.

I added, "I was in the office waiting for the waitress to get some more peanuts and I saw the price list. It's usually $500 to rent this room. How did you do it??"

Pop was a wreck. He looked to Alice again. "How much money have you got?"

"About $50," was her cool response. "You?" "Not enough!" Pop muttered. The panic was rising.

"Gimme your checkbook."

"Okay," agreed Alice. "I have it right . . . Oh, no. I left it home. On the vanity."

Pop looked to us. "You guys got any dough?"

We expected this. Pete pulled out about $18. I pulled out $11.

"You're welcome to all we have, Pop. How much did you expect to pay?"

"Two hundred bucks at the most."

I pulled Pete aside, and we held what looked like a very serious pow wow. We returned to Pop.

"Tell you what, Pop. Pete and I have our checkbooks in the car. Give us the $200 and we'll cover the rest." I think that's when we noticed he hadn't been breathing for the preceding thirty minutes. It was several months before Pete and I finally told him the truth. His response:

"I knew. I just went along. That'll be the day when you can put something over on your old man."

We love you, Pop.

TWENTY SIX –
Extracurricular Activities

The scripts kept getting better and the chemistry between all of us did the same. Ratings were good. Fan mail was coming in at a good clip. All was well at the ranch. As we fell into our various routines, we began to find time for other activities as well. Layouts, appearances, sports activities, trips, etc. I've included a few pictures pertaining to the aforementioned extracurricular activities.

The studios had put together a Hollywood softball league with teams made up of celebrities, agents, and PR guys from the industry. Jerry Lewis sponsored our team. And quite a team it was. Norm Alden, Mike Connors, Harvey Lembeck, Mickey Callan, me, Jack Palance, Peter Brown, Dennis Crosby (Bing's son), Pat Boone, and a few agents whose names escape me. Annette Funicello was one of our Bat Girls. This auspicious team would travel the country and play radio personalities from the various cities, usually playing them in that city's largest baseball stadium. Jack Palance and I were pitchers, and a formidable duo we were. If I wasn't pitching, I was in left field. People loved seeing us out of context. As a result, a lot of money was raised for a lot of good causes.

Then there was Comedy Diving, which I'd done since high school. I was invited several times to put on shows at various big-name hotels around town and occasionally in other cities. I did one

The Jerry Lewis-sponsored Hollywood
Celebrities Softball Team with Wenches

at the Beverly Hills Hotel. And to make sure it was a good show. I enrolled Pete and his good friend, Jeepers Bell, to perform with me.

Pete had worked with me before, and Jeepers, well, he was willing to do anything.

Pete, me and Jeepers Bell

The pool area was full but the attendees had not been told what to expect. The dressing room was at one end of the pool, the ten-foot diving board at the other. As Pete, Jeepers, and I were getting into costume, I laid out the plan. Jeepers would exit the dressing room first, whooping and hollering at the top of his lungs, running along the *left* side of the pool. Pete would do the same on the *right* side and I would follow Jeeper's path. When we reached the diving board we'd each do our first dive. We were set. Go! And Jeepers went, leaping over people in deck chairs

Pat and me.

"The mattress!!
Where's the mattress?!"

and bellowing at the top of his lungs. It wasn't until he reached the other end of the pool that he realized we weren't behind him. We were still in the dressing room watching him trying to explain his presence. Finally we appeared, yelling at him, demanding to know why he hadn't waited for us. It turned into a great routine, and were asked to come back again. Jeepers, too.

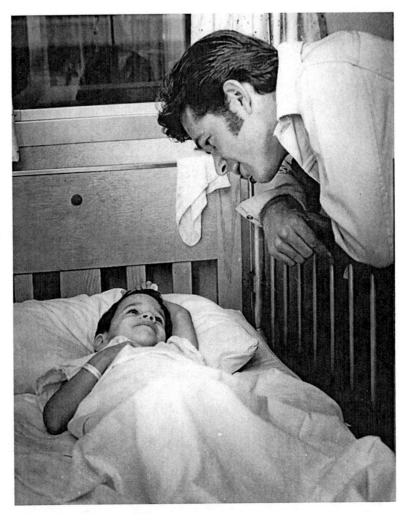

Gary at Dallas Children's Hospital. c. 1963

I ran track in high school, a pole vaulter, so of course if there was even the remotest chance of doing a magazine layout about track and field, I'd do it.

Visiting children's hospitals was emotionally tough for me. I visited a hospital ward in Dallas designed for terminally-ill children. I was dressed in my *Virginian* outfit, complete with gun and holster. The hospital officials were very gracious and grateful that I had agreed to include their ward in my itinerary. I told them I was the one who was honored. They warned me several times that if, at any time, I felt I needed a break, to just say so and we'd break.

We began and I had the opportunity to talk to thirty or forty kids, all of whom had little to no chance of surviving, for any number of reasons.

Never once did I see a tear or hear a complaint. Just smiles. We talked about all kinds of things, even what they wanted to do *if* they grew up. I guess I'd been in there for an hour or so when the director asked me to come with him. I followed him into the hall, and he asked if I was okay. "Sure," I said. "Why?" He said he just wanted to make sure, then asked me again if I was okay. I couldn't answer and looked at him for a long moment, then burst into tears. I sobbed, just mad that there was nothing I could do! The director said that I'd done more than I could ever imagine. I didn't see how. I got a drink of water, washed my face and we went back in, making sure we didn't missed anyone. Life is so precious, and its spirit so indomitable. I know I'll never forget that visit.

TWENTY SEVEN –
It's Feelin' Good

I liked being on a series. Especially this one. I wanted to make sure that everything stayed copacetic, so if anything negative reared its ugly head, I jumped on it. I wanted to handle it "right now" and get whatever it was out of the way and move on. I was also, understandably, more confident with myself and my position. Sometimes, a little "too confident" and "cocky" would show up.

With the second season well underway, Pat and I were now talking marriage. I initiated it. I didn't want to take any chances. God sent me an angel, and who was I to deny a gift from God? My problem was that I questioned how a girl like Pat could be interested in a guy like me. I carried that underlying doubt with me throughout our thirteen-year marriage. In retrospect, it all sounds so stupid. But that's the topic for my next book: *The Psychologically-Bent Side of Gary Clarke*. I'm taking advance orders now, and as soon as I have five, I'll write it.

Planning the wedding was great fun. Like where to get married. We were both Catholic, so that wasn't much of a problem. But there was one thing to consider: "Fan invasion." We were both starring on successful TV shows and there were fans. Were we to get married in Tinseltown, we were looking at the possibility of having the church overrun with hoards of people. So, what if we got married somewhere other than Hollywood? Another problem: We were buying a home at the top of Queens Road, right smack in the middle of Hollywood. A two-story home on a private drive at the end of a cul-de-sac. On a clear day, you could see Catalina from the side porch. We paid $60,000 for it. $60,000!! I checked its value five years ago: $750,000!!! We sold it in 1965 to Davey Jones of *The Monkees* for $66,000. Times certainly do change.

"Trust Me My Child!"

Because Blessed Sacrament Church, which was right smack in the middle of The Sunset Strip, was our parish, we were required to get married there. What to do? What to do?

Pat and I began looking for an alternative and we found one. A really nice church in Pasadena, California. Beautiful, off the beaten path, perfect. We talked to the priest, told him what we were up against and what we wanted to do. He felt fairly confident that the dilemma was easily surmountable and suggested that we meet with our parish priest, explain the situation, and more than likely we would get permission to marry outside our diocese.

Church interior in Pasadena, California. c. 1964

The following day, we met with one of the main priests of our parish. He was pleasant, warm, and gave us coffee while we chatted about the wedding. He listened to everything we had to say and agreed that our getting married at Blessed Sacrament could pose problems. He gave us the dispensation we needed with the stipulation that Pat return the following day to discuss the possibility of us having children and how we intended to raise them. We were happy. It had been much easier than we thought.

The next day and we're getting our new house ready to occupy. Pat left for her appointment and I went back to painting walls. An hour later she returns and she's as white as Doug's teeth. This wasn't like Pat. "What happened!!"

It seems that "our priest" could have cared less about any children we might have. His focus was on seducing Pat right there in his office. It even included the chasing around the desk routine. She only escaped by managing to punch him in the chest. Hard. He hesitated and she was out the door. "Son of a . . . . " I was headed out the door with killing on my mind. She grabbed me and got me to agree to wait while she called Monsignor Chris, her Father Confessor in Boston. I'd met Father Chris in New York a few months earlier when Pat was appearing at The Copacabana. I liked him and I trusted him. Pat related the incident to him and he responded, very calmly.

"Gary," was the first thing he said. "I know how you feel, but I'm asking you to trust me and to not do anything. Don't go see him. Don't call him. Can you do that?" I said I could.

"I'll take care of it. Give me a week," he continued. "I'll call you then."

Listening to Father Chris, I felt easier. A little. But had I run into that "priest" over the next few days . . . I don't know.

Father Chris called five days later. It seemed that this priest had made a habit of hitting on starlets who were about to get married, and in some cases been successful. I was mad again.

"But it's handled. As we speak, Father _____ is on his way to take on the conversion of a small native tribe in Brazil, somewhere near the headwaters of the Amazon. He is not expected to be recalled any time soon." And as far as I know, Father _____ is still there. Or at least his bones are.

It was a beautiful wedding (we'd spent a little more than my dad had). May 9th. A perfect day. Lots and lots of people attended. We tied the knot, the music started, and we marched up the aisle and out onto the church's large front landing. Pat and I were grinning at each other like kids when this bald man, about sixty, swooped in and enveloped Pat in a huge bear hug. Without thinking, she shoved him with all her might right into a brick wall.

"Pat!" he exclaimed. "It's me! Lee Cobb!" He wasn't wearing his toupee and Pat had never seen Lee without it.

She rushed up to him, threw her arms around his neck and hugged him for all she was worth. Lee laughed, I laughed, and Lee's wife, Mary, laughed the hardest. It was the first time we'd met Mary. What a sweet, sweet lady.

Up to that point, Pat and I had been working non-stop. Filmways, the company that produced *Petticoat Junction,* came up with a brainstorm that paid off. Using Pat ("Bobbie Jo") as the main vocal thrust, and adding Linda Kaye Henning ("Bettie Jo"), Jeannine Riley ("Billie Jo"), and Sheila James (of *Dobie Gillis* fame), they created The Ladybugs, a takeoff of The Beatles. They performed the Beatles song, "I Wanna Hold Your Hand" on a segment of *Petticoat Junction*. It went over so well that they were invited to appear on the *Ed Sullivan Show* (1965), a very big deal at the time. They were invited back again. It should probably be mentioned here that Ed had never once invited *me* on his show. Some say it was because he'd seen *The Tonight Show.* That theory was never confirmed.

I was getting more and more creative with "Steve's" character

Pat and "Ladybugs" in a scene from "Petticoat Junction." c. 1963

That's Pat, up front.

and kept trying out new things. Most of the time they worked; sometimes they didn't. I kept trying and did manage to keep things fresh. I began talking to our writers and directors to see if they could help me implement some of my ideas. They did all they could, but nothing new could be tried without being sanctioned by the producer, Frank Price. Frank and I had many a conversation pertaining to making Steve a little more prominent. Maybe another show or two where he was the main character. Or maybe give him a love inter-est. Frank wasn't buying any of it. The show had a particular thrust that only a few insiders knew about, and he didn't want to take the chance that some of their plans might be leaked to the competition. He was the producer and that was that. For him, maybe. Not for me.

Jeannine Riley, Pat, Ed Sullivan, Linda Kaye Henning, Sheila James

155

TWENTY EIGHT – The Beginning of the End

I mentioned Lew Wasserman earlier as the head of The Music Corporation of America (MCA), the head of Universal Studios, and my agent's father-in-law. It was the "my agent's father-in-law" part that led me to believe that Mr. Wasserman was the person to intercede on my behalf in my quest to bring a little more life to Steve's character.

His office—The Inner Sanctum—was housed in what was lovingly referred to as *The Black Tower*, a very dark, fifteen-story building that captured your eye from all else as you approached Universal Studios. Not many had been admitted to the Inner Sanctum, but I'd spoken to a few who had. They'd found it Impressive. Imposing. Intimidating. Still, setting my appointment with Mr. Wasserman was easier than I had been led to believe. I saw him the next day.

I arrived ten minutes early, and a very attractive and efficient secretary welcomed me with, "Good morning, Mr. Clarke. It's a pleasure to meet you. Mr. Wasserman is expecting you. This way please." She led me to a very tall set of double doors. I remember being impressed by how easily they opened.

"Mr. Clarke is here, sir."

"Gary. Please come in." His voice was pleasant, with a solid foundation of authority. He was tall, about 6' 1." Graying hair. Well-dressed in a dark suit and tie.

"Can I offer you something? Coffee. Tea. Coke. Wine. Ovaltine?"

I said a Pepsi would be fine.

"Diet?"

"I prefer leaded, if you have it."

"Two leaded Pepsies, Lana."

Lana. The perfect name for her.

Lew—he asked me to call him Lew—invited me to sit down. I did. Lana returned with the beverages and Lew took her aside, I assumed to let her know that he wasn't to be disturbed. I took the moment to take in this notorious, and sometimes feared, throne room. It was flawless. Everything was in harmony with everything else. The lighting, including the shadows, was meticulously set. Perfect paintings and tapestries perfectly placed. Furnishings were eclectic yet fit together perfectly. Even the aroma of the room was rich. I guessed that his desk alone must have cost thirty, forty bucks. I was an actor. What did I know?

We began. "I have two things I'd like to discuss with you, Lew."

"I'm all yours, Gary."

"You've probably heard that Pat Woodell and I are getting married."

"Yes. She seems like a wonderful young lady. Congratulations."

"Thank you. Well . . . we're buying a house and we need $5000 for the down payment. I was wondering if I might have an advance on my . . . . " He was out of his chair and on the phone.

"Lana, call finance and have them cut a check to Gary Clarke for $5000. Deliver it here in the next fifteen minutes."

"Thank you, Lew. I don't . . . . "

"It was a pleasure. I'm just glad I was able to help. What else can I do for you?" I proceeded to explain my "'Steve' situation."

We talked for thirty minutes with Lew listening respectfully to

Universal City's "Black Tower"

everything I had to say. Occasionally he'd ask a question, but mostly I did the talking. At the end, I was confident that I'd been heard. He stood, shook my hand, and invited me to drop in anytime. Leaving his office, I was walking on air. Lana had to stop me to give me my check.

Pat and I were married right after the end of the second season. We bought our house and moved in. It had a pool and a guest house. Very rustic with gables. And only one way in: the driveway. The other three sides of the house overlooked steep cliffs covered with trees and shrubs. We loved it.

The summer went on. I was invited to appear at a tourist attraction in Cherokee, North Carolina, a few miles west of Ashville. "Frontierland" provided gunfights, Indian raids on the fort, and a bevy of dancehall girls singing and dancing their hearts out in the saloon. My job was to meet and greet the tourists as "Steve Hill" and sign autographs. Cherokee, North Carolina was an Indian reservation. So, with the exception of the manager, his wife, and the cook—and me—everyone who worked at Frontierland was of Indian descent. Had a great time and made a few bucks.

The Real Scoop

Speaking of bucks, I was anxious to get back to work. Funds were getting low—new house expenses and all. Third season meant a bit of a raise in salary. I was excited. Till Ronnie, my agent, called.

"Gary, Universal didn't pick up your contract. Evidently you created some bad blood with a few executives."

"What are you talking about? Who? I met with Lew! Everything was fine. He even gave me the down payment for our home! Talk to . . . . "

"I did," Ronnie interrupted. "He said that the decisions for what happens on *The Virginian* is totally up to the producer, and Frank decided not to renew your contract."

"That's it?" I asked. "There's nothing you or Lew can do?"

"It's not up to Lew and I've done everything I can. Sorry, Gary."

I've been asked more times than I care to remember why I "left the show." I didn't leave. I was fired. I believe that the reasons I was fired were these: I got a little too pushy, too cocky for the powers that be. That can always be a problem, or at least an indication of future problems.

Also, I went over the producer's head. That's always a no-no. Even if Lew agreed 100% with what I had to say, for him to side with me over Frank would have set a very dangerous precedent. Lew's office would have been inundated with whiney, unhappy, and discontented actors. And there is nothing more annoying than a whiney, unhappy, and discontented actor. No. Lew had to side with Frank. Lesson learned. And that, dear friends, is how it happened.

Ironically, they brought my character back three times in the third season, paying me four times what my contract salary would've been. Who'd 'a thought?

TWENTY NINE –
Life After *The Virginian*

Ronnie Leif lost interest after that, which left me agentless. But things just kept chugging along. Oh, there were those moments of embarrassment when people would ask what happened, but you rolled with it—or you'd hibernate.

Some months later, Steve Ihnat recommended me for a pilot he was doing with Gene Roddenberry. It was called *Police Story*, and Steve and I were to be detective partners. But, as the fates would have it, it didn't sell. Put a few shekels in the coffers, though.

Pat And Jack

The months passed and work started to pick up—for me *and* Pat. Her new manager, Irving Fein, also happened to manage Jack Benny (not too shabby), and he set up an audition for Pat to sing for Jack. She sang and Jack signed her on the spot to tour the US and Canada with his show, singing and doing skits with him. A few weeks of rehearsal, musical arrangements, wardrobe, and *The Jack Benny Show* was on the road.

I caught up with them in Alberta, Canada. Pat and I were in the coffee shop before the show and we spotted Richard Prior. We'd met Richard a few times in L.A. He'd been doing the Hollywood circuit of small clubs, and we'd catch him whenever we could. He had a club date in Alberta, saw that Pat was working with Jack, and came to see the show. Pat invited him to come backstage after the show to meet Jack. Richard was a little nervous about intruding on "Jack Benny," but with a little coaxing, he finally came 'round.

"Sure, singing for Jack Benny may have helped, but this is the shot that really clinched the deal for her."

Richard and I watched the show together, made our way backstage, and Irving invited us in. Jack was relaxing in his robe as introductions were made, his "deadpan" very much in evidence. Pat and I knew the routine. Richard didn't and had second thoughts about ever accepting Pat's invite to come backstage. Trying to put him at ease, Pat and I raved about Richard and some of his routines. At one point, in the midst of our ranting about Richard's talents, Jack, with his perfect timing, said, "Well... you know... I'm a comedian, too." We laughed. Richard was sure Jack hated him. After much cajoling, we convinced Richard to do his "Rumplestilpskin" (spelling is correct) routine. And he did. Better than we'd ever seen it before. We were laughing tears by the time he finished. Jack was still deadpan. He just looked at Richard. The laughter died down, and a tense, pregnant silence followed. Interminable. Richard was sweating, knowing he had just bombed in front of one of the world's most famous comedians. Finally, without a word, Jack stood and headed for his private dressing room. He stopped in the doorway, flipped up his robe, and *mooned* the entire room. And the door slammed behind him. It took a while for Pat and Irving to convince Richard that he would never receive a finer, or higher compliment than a *mooning* from Jack Benny. As they say in "mob lingo," Richard Prior had been "made."

L'scribe is Born

Necessity is the mother of invention, and God has plans for us. My seemingly inopportune departure from *El Virginian* and the end of the run for *Hondo* presented me with an unsuspected windfall which happened during a lunch with Bill Kiley, a friend of mine whom I'd met when he was NBC's liaison to *The Virginian*. Now he was the head of NBC publicity. We ate, we talked, we reminisced. At one point, Bill mentioned a new show they had in the works. A comedy about a bumbling spy called *Get Smart*. He spoke, I listened. At the end of the conversation, I told him that I had an idea for a segment. Bill said to write it up, get it to him, and he'd see what he could do.

I didn't have a typewriter, and money was still a bit tight. Undaunted, I bought an old Underwood Noiseless Typewriter from The Salvation Army for $15 and had it overhauled for $20. Bought a tiny desk for $10 at a yard sale, and I was set to go. I wrote like crazy, and in four days, I'd finished a half-hour shooting script for *Get Smart*. When Bill read it, he said he thought it was right down *Get Smart*'s alley.

"But the production company's not taking any unsolicited scripts." That meant if you weren't a known writer, and the *Get Smart* people hadn't hired you to write a script, they wouldn't read it. *Drat!!*

I told my then agent, Phil Gittleman, what Bill had said about the script *and* what he had said about "unsolicited scripts." Phil said, "Let me take a crack at it. I know a couple of guys at *Get Smart*." Then, a dark cloud materialized over my head and I remembered something I had been told while working on *Hondo*. I had presented an outline for a segment of *Hondo* to Andy Fenady, the producer. He took it from me, held it for about three seconds, then handed it back accompanied by these profound words of wisdom:

"Gary. You're an actor. Actors don't write, they act. Let the writers write." I believed him.

Yep, I bought it. After all, he was a *producer*. I was naught but a lowly actor. Anyway, what he said stuck.

A solution flashed before us! When Phil submitted my script to the *Get Smart* group, the writing credit would read: Written by Clarke F. L'Amoreaux, my real name. Phil said, "I think it'll work." And off he went to make it work.

Universal had called on me again (couldn't live without me) to star in a movie called *Wild, Wild Winter*, a "Beach Party" movie in the snow that was to be shot at a Lake Tahoe ski resort. Pat and I discussed what we might do should the *Get Smart* people read my script, like it, and want to get in touch with me. They could call me in Tahoe, but the movie company would have me listed as Gary Clarke. Another solution flashed! I would register at the hotel under *both* names, which I did. And a good thing, too. I wasn't there more than two days when "Clarke L'Amoreaux" received a call from the head writer for *Get Smart*. A very good sign because they *never* call you to say they *don't* want your script; only when they do. I was smiling.

"Clarke?" he began. "This is Buck Henry. I'm one of the writers for *Get Smart*." *One* of the writers?! How about *head* writer and co-creator with Mel Brooks.

"It's a pleasure, Mr. Henry."

"We've read your script and like it very much. When can we meet?"

I told him I'd be back in a week, we set a time, I assured him I'd be there, and the call was over. It looked like I'd sold my script, not to just anyone, but to Buck Henry and Mel Brooks! I was bouncing off the walls when I called Pat to give her the good news. I actually bounced for a while—until she asked a very important question: "What if they recognize you?" Andy Fenady's dictate rang in my

Wild, Wild Winter movie poster c. 1965

Maxwell Smart,
Agent 99 and Hymie

ears: "Writers write. Actors act." Crap! There must be something I can do.

Over the next several days a plan emerged, and by meeting time it had been fully implemented. A disguise. Frumpy clothes (most writers looked frumpy), glasses (which I hadn't worn till then) and hair parted in the middle. I also added a slightly higher voice. It worked. They bought my script. I'd fooled them!! They had especially liked the character I created: "Hymie, the robot," a human-looking robot (played by Dick Gautier) who obeyed all commands literally: "Hymie, lend me a hand," which prompted Hymie to unscrew his hand and give it to you.

There were three things that were particularly rewarding in seeing my script come to life. Like walking on the set the first day and seeing the laboratory reconstructed exactly as I had written it. And, of course, seeing my name under the "Written by" credit. I think my favorite was the "gorilla guy." I'd written in the part of a gorilla who was to wrestle Hymie. And there he was. A guy in a gorilla suit, sitting with a group of extras, holding his gorilla head in his arm. No one on the set knew me from Adam, so I could just stand around and watch and listen. The gorilla guy was talking:

"My wife and I have been talking about taking the kids to Yosemite Park for years now. You know, camp out and stuff. We'd given up until I got the call for this job. Now we can do it! We're leaving Saturday morning. Kids are packed already."

I wanted to tap him on the shoulder and tell him that I remember the exact moment I decided to write in the gorilla. I didn't, but it was really a very rewarding moment. I'm sure they had fun.

The segment, called "Back To The Old Drawing Board," turned out very well, and they asked me to write another. Then another. By the time I'd written the third script, I was beginning to feel a little strange about my "double life." I'd been working for them for a few months. They liked my work, so what difference would it make if I *was* an actor? None. Nope. I didn't like it. Not at all. As with Lee J. Cobb, I had to do something.

Foregoing my usual disguise, I knocked on Buck Henry's office door and asked if he had a minute.

"Sure, Clarke. C'mon in. Loved the last script."

"Great. Thanks."

"What can I do for you?"

"Well," I stumbled. "I want to get something straight. First off, I love working with you and Mel and Don."

"We're glad to have you. Is there a problem?

"I hope not. It's just . . . well, I haven't been straight with you."

"Oh?"

"You see, I am Clarke L'Amoreaux. It's my real name."

"Uh huh."

"But I'm also Gary Clarke. An actor. I've been in a lot of stuff."

"Yeah," said Buck. "We know."

"What?! You know?"

"Sure. We watch television, too."

"But . . . why didn't you say anything?"

"Wanted to see how far you'd go."

I told him the Andy Fenady story. He laughed, I laughed, and as I was leaving he said, "You know, Gary. For an actor you write a hell of a script."

Hondo

About a year after my departure from *The Virginian* I received a call from MGM. I was up for a new Western series they were doing called *Hondo*, based on the John Wayne movie. Short version is that agents, producers, and directors got together, and I got the part of "Captain Richards." Ralph Taeger was to play the title role. Other regulars included Noah Berry, Jr. (whom they called "Pidge"), Michael Pate, William Bryant, and Kathie Browne.

Ralph Taeger and I had never met, but we did have a history. It seems that several years before, he had had a major crush on Connie Stevens at a time when Connie and I were hot and heavy. On this particular day, it just so happened that Kelly Gordon and I were visiting Connie and her dad, Teddy Stevens, in their home just outside Hollywood.

I had fallen asleep on a couch at the back of the house when the doorbell rang. I heard nothing. Connie answered the door (all this was told to me later). It was Ralph, feverish with passion, wanting to know why Connie wouldn't go out with him. Attempting to calm him, Teddy invited him in, offering him a Coke, iced tea, or a sedative. He declined all. In answer to his question, Connie told him that she and I were going to be married and that dating was out of the question.

Ralph posed a possibility: "What if Gary was out of the picture? Would you go out with me then?"

"But he isn't," Connie shot back brilliantly.

Kelly and Teddy sat at the ready.

"I could arrange it," Ralph promised.

It took the three of them to get him to the point where it was safe to let him out among the citizenry. He apologized for the intrusion, and that was that. I think he was engaged to someone else a week later.

Ralph and the horse he rode in on.

Let me point out a few things about Ralph Taeger. He was big, he was strong, and the word "pain" was not in his vocabulary. He was one of a very few people I've met that actually had muscles in their hair. Had not my Guardian Angel known about Ralph's visit to Connie's beforehand and had me fall asleep on a couch in the back of the house, and had I been in the living room when Ralph was admitted, you would not be reading these words now. That's all I have to say.

With my penchant for wanting to "keep thing above board," I related that story to Ralph on the first day of shooting. Best to establish what our relationship was going to be from the get-go. He remembered the incident—vaguely. He thanked me for telling him and said he was looking forward to working with me. From that moment on, we were fast friends.

However, Ralph did have a few quirks. Allow me to elucidate. The town where we shot most of the interiors was built on a large sound stage at MGM Studios, complete with a general store, sheriff's office, jail, livery stable, hotel, etc. They had brought in tons of dirt to lay down for the streets. In fact, almost the entire sound stage was covered with a thick layer of dirt.

We'd shot the first two or three shows, and it seemed that Ralph was in virtually every scene. He had time to do little else. Lunch was usually taken on the set, at least for him. Even bathroom breaks caused an unwanted delay in shooting, mainly because the nearest bathroom was two blocks away and getting there, doing your business, and getting back took time! Ralph found a solution. Whenever he had to relieve himself, he'd go around to the back of one set or another, find an out-of-the-way mound of dirt, and "mark" it. Only a very few of us knew at first, but things like that have a way of getting 'round.

One day, a reporter, a lady reporter, came on the set to interview Ralph. He was always doing interviews. She asked the assistant director where Ralph was. He said he didn't know. But I did, and I told her.

"He's right around back there, miss," I said, indicating an out-of-the-way store front.

She thanked me and followed my directions. She found him. He was in the midst of "marking" another dirt mound, which she at first failed to notice. She had launched into why she was there when what Ralph was doing finally registered. Stopped her cold. Ralph, smiling calmly at her, said he'd be with her in a moment. We never saw her again.

Even the deepest, darkest secrets fall apart in the cold light of day, and Ralph's was no exception. Word had definitely gotten out. Way out.

One mid-morning, we had three visitors on the set. Three men who rarely visited sets. James Aubrey, the head of the studio, the head of the TV division (forgot his name), and Andy Fenady, the producer of the show itself. The hubub on the set quieted as the trio approached.

"Was the show canceled?" we muttered. "Did someone die?" "Maybe John Wayne was going to be a guest star!" We all, as incon-

In case you've forgotten – it's me.

spicuously as possible, followed them as they zeroed in on Ralph. Then Ralph and three of some of the most powerful men in the motion picture industry had the following conversation:

Fenady:	Good morning, Ralph.
Ralph:	Gentlemen.
Aubrey:	Ralph, you've got to stop peeing in the dirt!
TV Head:	People are complaining.
Fenady:	It's unsanitary.
Aubrey:	Fan magazines are talking about it.
Ralph:	Really?
Fenady:	Yes!
Ralph:	I don't pee just anywhere. I have regular places that . . . .
TV Head:	That's beside the point! It just isn't done!
Aubrey:	I have better things to do that discuss your peeing peculiarities.

Fenady: You just can't do it, Ralph.

TV Head: People could get sick. Even die.

Fenady: Just stop it, Ralph.

Aubrey: Enough said. I never want to have this discussion again.

And off they walked. The "pee" conversation was over, and Ralph watched calmly as they left. Pidge and I moved in, flanking the pee-baby. "Waddya gonna do, Ralph."

"I don't know. If they don't give me time to . . . What do they expect me to do, pee my pants? Is that what they . . . Hmm!" And he peed his pants. Right where he stood. The water trail stretching from crotch to mid-calf.

The "pee-the-pants" thing happened several times over the following week, usually as a joke. Then one day, a very irate wardrobe guy pulled me aside. I don't remember his name, so let's call him Bob. He was this sweet and very efficient gay person who took great pride in handling all of the men's wardrobe.

"Gary," he said. "I'm at my wit's end. I am seriously thinking about quitting!"

"Why?" I asked. I couldn't imagine.

"It's Ralph," he went on. "It's disgusting. There were six pairs of 'pissy' pants on the floor in his dressing room. He just leaves them there for me to pick up and have cleaned. I just can't take anymore."

I sympathized. "Have you talked to him?"

"No. He's the star. I'm just a . . . Do you think it would do any good?"

"Ralph's a reasonable guy. What have you got to lose?"

He said he'd talk to him at the first opportunity. I got to Ralph and warned him of the impending confrontation. He promised he'd take care of it. He did. Bob did his best to keep it together when he finally spoke to Ralph, but it was clear that he was hanging on by a thread, a frayed one at that. Ralph listened compassionately, then when Bob was finished, spent, if you will, Ralph *lied through his teeth*.

"I'm really sorry, Bob. I should have said something earlier. I was embarrassed. Afraid I might lose my job. But it's only fair that I tell you. I hope you'll understand. You see, it's like this. I only get a twenty-second warning before . . . you know. I try to get somewhere where I can . . . you know, and there are times that I don't make it, then I . . . you know. I just don't know what to do." Bob was moved to tears.

"Oh, Ralphie, don't you worry about a thing. I'll take care of it. And you can be sure that no one will ever hear about . . . you know, from me."

And he was gone. When Ralphie got to his dressing room the next morning he found six pairs of "Hondo" pants hanging neatly in his closet, and two oversized, sand-filled litter boxes for him to . . . you know, in. The "pissy" pants issue never came up again.

THIRTY – *Tempus Fugit*

Time *does* fly, whether you're having fun or not. In my case, it flew by very fast. Days into weeks into months into years. Somewhere during the few years following *Hondo*, there was a Screen Actors Guild strike and no one was working. So, if you're not working in your chosen profession, you find something else. Been there, done that, I could do it again.

I sold cable TV door-to-door for a few months. It was okay. Encyclopedias were next. Not your run-of-the-mill encyclopedias, but *Negro Heritage Library* encyclopedias: The first comprehensive compilation of Black history, complete in twenty volumes. $10 down, $10 per month. These, too, were sold door-to-door. By a White guy. In Watts. At night. Alone. Believe it or not, the response was great.

Did that for several months. My next job, also door-to-door, was selling *more* encyclopedias, this time regular encyclopedias, but with an incentive. If you bought a set of *these* encyclopedias, you would also receive *two* of the following: a big white leather-bound family bible; a set of authentic pots and pans; a ninety-eight-piece tool kit; a one-year subscription to *Horizon* magazine; A *Betty Crocker Cook Book*; a real hand-painted tablecloth imported all the way from Tijuana, Mexico; a set of bookends made out of real horseshoes; a 15% discount off a *Famous Artists Art Course;* and a thirty-two-piece set of genuine 100% metal dinnerware. Like I said, you gotta do what you gotta do.

est

A few years later, found Pat and me working in San Francisco for "est:" an educational corporation. (Yep. Slowed up for Pat, too.) A two-weekend self-help seminar. There was/is much controversy surrounding these seminars, usually fostered by people who had no idea what it was all about. Not unlike our political system today. Personally, I found it very valuable in my life. I eventually wound up as Managing Editor of their monthly periodical, *The Graduate Review*, which was read around the world. I got to travel the country, Europe, Hawaii—even spent four days in San Quentin Prison where we did a seminar for the inmates. Now *that's* something we could spend a little time on.

My job, along with managing the production of the paper, was to write articles about the people and events associated with est. At one point my boss told me, and I found it hard to get my mind around the idea, that my articles, over seventy-five, were being read around the world by over a million people, which may be true, but never once did any of those readers call, write, send an email, nothing! A little acknowledgement would have been appreciated, y'know.

Didn't have to be a lot. Something simple. A buck-and-a-half would've been fine. Some people just don't care. But far be it from me to hold a grudge. But I would be remiss if I didn't say, "What goes around comes around." 'Nuff said.

Gary and Pat near the end.
c. 1978

My thirteen-year marriage to Pat ended in San Francisco. Some might call our divorce strange. It was different, I'll give you that. Different in that we didn't hate each other or wish each other ill. We even used the same divorce attorney. Two years later, when Pat remarried, I was one of the ushers. Then, when Jerrene and I got married, Pat helped her put her wardrobe together, and Vern, her husband, was my best man. I look at it like this: You loved each other when you got married. Is it absolutely necessary to hate each other in order to get a divorce? I'd done that with my first wife and *that* sure didn't work out.

Footloose And Fancy Free

Having moved back to L.A., I spent some of my time finding another agent and looking for work as an actor. Mostly I was finishing a script that I'd started in San Francisco. Just looking for inroads. There were good times, there were bad times, you know, like life. Despite everything, my Guardian Angel never left my side. I know. You're going to ask me how I know. I just know, y'know. And they (there's more than one) told me that there'd be naysayers and that I should be prepared. So I took some snapshots. Videos. Selfies. Of me and my angels. Some great shots. I was creating a pile of proof. And it worked—for a while. They . . . well . . . they started to fade. Not the whole picture, just the angels. My images stayed fine. I asked my angels why they fade and they told me that even if I were to show them to people as proof, they would all probably say they were Photoshopped.

And Yet Another Career

Nothing was happening in the entertainment industry, for me and many others. Ebb and flow is common in our business. Time to start looking again. I was hoping against hope to find something other than encyclopedias.

Vern (Pat's husband) was in commercial real estate and was looking to branch out into residential. He was considering Phoenix,

Arizona for his initial thrust, and he and Pat invited me to go with them as they checked out the territory. I liked Phoenix. It was hot, but I liked it. As for Vern, he found the territory very fertile and decided Phoenix was where he wanted to invest his energy. We were in conversation for the next several days. He wanted me to move to Phoenix and spearhead his residential real estate business. I wanted to

Vern and his Rottweiler, "Fang."

stay in Hollywood where my work was. He reminded me (accurately, I might add) that there hadn't been any of *my* work for the past year. He was right, which reminded me of the story about the actor who hadn't had an acting job in ten years when his friend found him shoveling elephant poop at a Barnum & Bailey's Circus.

"Clive," he said. "You don't have to do this! Come with me and I'll make you a partner in my accounting firm."

"What?!" exclaimed Clive. "And give up show business??"

Two weeks later, I was on my way to Phoenix. Vern and I bought sixty-one homes, fixed them up, and turned them. As the fates would have it, I also found an agent who bombarded me with auditions and interviews, which resulted in a bunch of commercials, TV shows, and movies. And, *and*, I found Jerrene. Met in April, married in October. Okay. Now I get to tell one on Jerrene.

I knew almost immediately that she was the one for me. She, on the other hand, had never, ever thought of even considering a relationship with (ugh!) an actor. Fortunately for me, I was selling real estate when we met, so she assumed that I was a realtor who only "dabbled" in acting from time to time. And I did nothing to correct her assumption. We dated, fell in love, and soon began discussing marriage. It was a wonderful courtship. Watching her smile was heaven. Watching and hearing her laugh was beyond even that. One night, I don't remember when, she casually asked how old I was.

"How old do you think I am?"

"Ohh . . . forty-five?" she ventured.

Five minutes after "I do."

"Good guess," I lied. I was fifty-six. Jerrene was thirty.

She told me later that her first thought was, *Forty-five. Hmm. Well, at least he's younger than my parents.*

A few months later, when our marriage was imminent and it was absolutely inappropriate to carry the lie any further, I said, "Honey, there's something I've got to tell you."

Oh, my God, she thought. *He's married!*

But with amazing calmness she simply said, "Oh? What?"

"I'm not forty-five."

Strange, she thought. *Why would anyone lie about being younger?*

"I'm fifty-six."

She took it quite well. Other than her eyes rolling back into her head and the rapid body convulsions, she did fine. I jumped right in with a solution.

"So here's what we'll do. This had to be a shock, so you're going to need some time to think about what I've said. We'll take a week, maybe ten days. You mull it over. We won't talk to or see each other. If you want to go out, date someone else, then you should. All I ask is that when you've thought about it, you give me a call and let me know. If this won't work for you then it's best that we know now. I know where I stand, but you've got to be sure."

And for eight days we didn't see each other or talk to one another. Around day five, I found a dress she'd left at my house. I wrapped it as a gift and returned it to her office, first making sure she wasn't there. I'd enclosed a note. I left it on her desk and that was all. Finally, when eight days had elapsed, she called.

J —

I WORE THIS ONCE. IT LOOKED GOOD ON ME, BUT IT LOOKS BETTER ON YOU.

JUST A LITTLE BETTER. BUT NEVERTHELESS . . . BETTER.

G

The original. I didn't know she'd kept it.

"Hi."

"Hi," I responded glibly. "How are you?"

"Good," she said. "You?"

"Pretty good. Keeping busy."

"Me, too. It's been kind of . . . . "

I interrupted. "What have you decided?" She paused a moment then said:

"I've decided that I *don't* want to spend the rest of my life without you." And that, dear friends, was that. I was hooked, landed, thrown in the pan, and fried to a crisp. I knew from the start that she was the one, and now God and the fates had proven it.

Back On The Boards

Then, suddenly, I'm working all the time (remember the "feast or famine" thing?) doing TV shows, movies for television, regular movies, commercials, etc. My agent sent me to Tucson to interview for a Western movie written by Kevin Jarre who was also designated to direct the epic. Kevin also wrote *Glory,* a Civil War saga, and *Rambo: First Blood.* There were others, but you get the idea.

Jerrene drove with me to a motel in Tucson where casting was being held. When we got there, we found a hundred guys waiting outdoors to audition for various parts. It was hot, very hot, *and* Kevin was late getting back from lunch. He returned, and I told Jerrene that she might want to go and get something cool to drink because it looked like it would be quite a while before they got to me. No sooner were the words out of my mouth than Holly Hire, the lady in charge of casting, called me right to the front of the line. Didn't know why, but I couldn't refuse a lady. I went in to meet Kevin. He was pleasant, a bit distant, but complimentary about my reading. Holly and I were talking quietly as he looked over my resume. Then, suddenly: "I knew I recognized you!" he blurted. "You were Cap-

Kurt catches me trying to steal his watch.
I just wanted to look at it. Really.

On my resume: "I saved Bill Paxton's ass!"

tain Richards on *Hondo*! I *loved* the way you played that character! Perfect! Absolutely perfect!" The phone rang. He picked it up and spoke into it for a few minutes. Holly leaned over and whispered to me, a twinkle in her voice, "I think you've got the part." I did, and I was booked for fifteen weeks! The movie was *Tombstone* (1993). Kurt Russell. Sam Elliott. Bill Paxton. Val Kilmer. What a cast.

Making friends with these guys was so natural and easy. Kurt reminded me that I had worked with his dad, Bing Russell, several times on *The Virginian*, and said that his dad had spoken of me often. Bill Paxton was a hoot. He mentioned to me that he had a rash and it was killing him. I said I had an ointment in my dopp kit that might help. He accepted it gratefully. I can't tell you where the rash was, but the next morning he came up to me, gave me a hug and said, "Gary. You saved my ass."

Temperatures were in the hundreds. I mean it was hot. Very hot. People were passing out. Who wouldn't, wearing those heavy woolen period costumes? The company doctor almost shut down shooting because of the heat. Extra water and canopies were brought in and that seemed to cool people down. You see, when you're shooting, in the sun, under those hot lights, you only have a few minutes before your hair starts to smoke. But everyone, I mean everyone, was a complete professional. If anyone whined or complained, I didn't hear about it. In the midst of all this was Sam Elliott. Quiet, professional, unassuming, a gentleman. Except when he was in character—then, a powerhouse. On this particular day, we were shooting at the

Two months till Ava

train station where it was about 110 in the shade, of which there was little.

Jerrene had come to the set with me (she loved to watch the shooting) and had already met Kurt, Goldie Hawn, who happened to be visiting Kurt, and Bill. She had been given a director's chair and a nice spot under one of the canopies, which was good because

Sam Elliott and me. An honor and a privilege.

she was seven months pregnant with Ava. And *everyone* made sure she always had plenty of water. Sam was the only one she hadn't met, and we spotted him about thirty yards away, standing by the train in a tiny patch of shade. All by himself, waiting for the next scene.

"Do you think he'd mind if I went over and told him how much I've enjoyed his work?" Jerrene wondered. "I'm sure he wouldn't," I replied. "I'll go ask and make sure he's not going over his lines or something."

I walked over.

"Sam?" We'd already met. "Would you mind if my wife came over and said hello? She's been a fan. . . . "

"Not in this heat. Why don't we go over there?" We walked over, Sam introduced himself, and they chatted, about . . . stuff, for forty-five minutes, as if they'd been friends forever.

Much of the credit for the success of this film goes to Kurt Russell. The man is a complete professional and his fingerprint was all over this production. *Tombstone* has become a classic. I am proud to have been a part of it.

The Big 6 – 0

Through the years, friends and family have found it very difficult to surprise me. I just have a sense of when someone's about to try to put one over on me. Perhaps I should say *most* of the time I have a sense.

It all began about two months before *Tombstone*. I was home, in Phoenix, working in my office. The phone rang and I answered it. It was a director friend of mine calling from L.A.

"Jerry!" I said. "To what do I owe the pleasure?"

He explained: "I got a note from Jerrene about your birthday party and I wanted to let her know that I wouldn't be able to make it. I'm starting a new flick. I'll be there is spirit, though."

A birthday party? For me? First *I'd* heard about it. I mentioned the call to Jerrene but didn't make a big deal out of it. She'd known how hard it was to surprise me and now probably knew that I knew. I let it go, figuring that I'd go along with whatever she had planned so as not to spoil anything.

About two weeks later, Jerrene and I were heading out for an early movie when she reminded me that we were to have dinner with John and Paige Jackson at their house. I looked at her. She didn't look back.

"How many are going to be there?" I asked knowingly.

She got that "Oh-damn-I've-been-found-out" expression on her face.

"About twenty-five or thirty," she admitted reluctantly.

"Wow. That many?" I responded.

"Maybe more," she added.

I assured her I'd play along. She was happy and her plan unfolded. No sooner had we pulled up in front of the house than a dozen of our friends swarmed the car, pulled me out, sat me in a wheelchair, covered my lap with a shawl and wheeled me into the house.

A large, homemade, "colored-outside-the-lines banner" announcing "The First Annual Gary Clarke Film Festival" greeted me as we entered. Under the sign was a small black and white TV. It was on and *Dragstrip Riot* was playing.

They wheeled me past the TV to a dining room table upon which sat my birthday cake—baked in the shape of—yes, a wheelchair! Then into the kitchen, where I was handed as tumbler full of the worst champagne I'd ever tasted, and I have tasted some *bad* champagne. A second, small, black and white television was on and playing *Missile to the Moon*.

Back into the living room, a well-meaning but bad rendition of "Happy Birthday" and an opportunity to blow out sixty candles,

My son, Dave, and me.

most of which had melted onto the chocolate cake's white icing. I couldn't have blown out sixty candles when I was twenty!! This was followed up with the obligatory opening of "gifts for an Old Guy:" a bed pan; a cane with a horn attached; a dozen cans of Ensure; Depends; laxatives; Preparation H; and my favorite, a little device that, when the button was pushed, would call out: "Help! I've fallen and I can't get up!!"

We all laughed, I went along for the ride, it was fun and funny and, without a doubt, the tackiest, cheesiest birthday party, mine or anybody else's, I had ever experienced. During the "party," I'd received several phone calls from people—my brothers, my mother, Pat and Vern—apologizing profusely for not being able to attend. I said that it was okay and I'd send them pictures. Jerrene apologized for the tackiness. "But you have to admit, it was fun!"

Meanwhile, Dave (my son) and I had just finished producing a fundraiser for The Make-a-Wish Foundation, something we'd done annually over the preceding six years. One of the sponsors for the Foundation was Joe Arpaio's Sheriff's Department. Dave was one of the Department's police officers, and I was Dave's dad, which made it fairly inevitable that I would meet Arpaio himself. I did and we hit it off. I liked his tough, no-nonsense style. He actually wanted me to write a movie about his life. I said sure, and that the going rate for a completed screenplay was about $50,000. He said he'd get back to me. Still waiting.

Dave came to me and said he was to receive a commendation from Arpaio for some "above and beyond the call of duty" incident he had handled while he was on duty at the city jail. It seems that an inmate got hold of a knife and was threatening another officer. Dave took him down and relieved him of the "blade."

So now Dave was to get the award and make a speech. He asked if Jerrene and I would go with him, his wife, Marie, and his son, Matthew (10), for moral support. I said "absolutely." And I even offered to help him with his speech.

"Speech? What. . . . Oh, yeah. The speech." He said he'd like me to read what he had written. He got it to me a few days later. It was terrible! It read like he'd written it as an afterthought while sitting in the john. I told him I'd tweak it a little.

Gary and Jerrene at the GC Festival c. 1993.

Jerrene and I decided that we wanted to make this a special event for Dave. He was going to wear a tux; I would, too. And a limousine! Let's pick up his family and him in a limo! They'd love it. Jerrene said she'd arrange it.

Came "The Evening." The limo arrived, and I gave the driver specific instructions on how to act and what to say when we picked up Dave and family. He said he understood. We got to the house, he knocked on the door, and Dave, Marie, and Matthew came out. The driver indicated the limo. I expected a "Wow! A limo! Holy Moly!" or something. I got little to nothing. I chalked it up to Dave being nervous about the award and the speech. Well, no need to worry about the speech. I'd written a great one. I'd even brought a tape recorder to record this momentous moment. I knew it would be something Dave would cherish forever. And I'd written it. I figured that when Arpaio found out that I'd written Dave's speech, he'd put me on the payroll to write all of his.

We're on the road to the fancy Scottsdale Hotel and Dave's award. By now they commented on the limo. I thought maybe Jerrene had given them the high sign, because it did happen rather abruptly. That was alright. Nerves. But wait. We'd just driven past the hotel. I pointed it out to the driver who calmly replied, "We're a little early so I thought I'd take the long way." What "long way?" And how did *he* know we were early? Did Dave tell him? If so, when? Jerrene must have seen my consternation and told me that she had told the driver. Yeah? When? Well . . . Dave told her. Yeah? When?? I had missed something. Never mind.

This would be an opportunity for Dave to read over his speech. He said he didn't need to. I said I'd made several changes from his original. He said he didn't need to. I said that there would be dignitaries in the audience. He said he didn't need to. I shoved the speech at him. He took it. He took it, crumpled it up and threw it out the window just as the limo came to a stop.

A "Happy 60ᵗʰ Birthday" at the GC Film Festival

As I watched the speech, my incredibly well-written speech, bounce onto the sidewalk, I noticed that we had stopped in front of a Harkins movie theater, where a couple of hundred fancy dressed people were gathered and all seemed to be looking our way. I'm confused. Jerrene pointed up to the marquee that announced in very bold letters: "Gary Clarke Film Festival."

The driver, smiling, opened the back door and offered me his hand. I took it, got out and a deafening roar of cheering and yelling erupted from the crowd. "What the. . . . " It was still a blur. Jamie McFerren, a news anchor friend of ours, approached me and held up a microphone.

"Happy birthday, Gary. Welcome to the Gary Clarke Film Festival. This is your night."

And it was. It really was. Jerrene had gotten me good. I mean good!! I didn't have a clue. The call from the L.A. director had been an accident and almost blew the two months work that Jerrene, Dave, and a hundred others had already put in. The "tacky birthday

And the best years were yet to come c. 1993

party" had been thrown together to make me think that *that* had been my surprise party all along. It worked, and that's exactly what I thought. Dave's "commendation" dinner and speech was a way to get me into a tux and out of the house. The limo driver was just one of the "Put-the-party-together" group. He had driven the route from Dave's house to the theater a dozen times just to make sure his part coordinated with the rest of the plan.

Evidently, whenever I was out of the house, working or whatever, Jerrene would go through my phone book, get addresses and send out invitations. RSVP's were made to a friend's office. If there were questions, a phone number would be taken and Jerrene would return the call. She was the magical hub of it all.

People, friends I hadn't seen for years, flew in from all over the country and were there for *my* birthday. Jerrene and I moved up through the screaming crowd. I shook hands, signed autographs

Me, brother Mike, Mom and Pete

and hugged a lot. We were all ushered into the largest theater of this particular Harkin's complex. It was, in fact, where Dan Harkins (the theater owner) and his wife were married ten years before.

Dave MC'd the evening and for two hours introduced friend after friend and family member after family member. Friends who couldn't make it sent videos which were played. Connie sent one, as did Dick Gautier (Hymie on *Get Smart*). Doug McClure and Burt Reynolds did one together. One of my favorites was from Jerry Beatty, Jerrene's dad, who said, "I always knew that Jerrene might marry someone older, but I didn't know he'd be older than *me* . . . and *prettier!!*"

The movie theater event was only the first half. Attendees were given directions to the second half of the event, which was to take place on the top floor of the Bank One building, then the tallest structure in Phoenix.

Our limo pulled into the parking area and we were greeted by a young man wearing tuxedo tails who then directed us to the elevator. We took the elevator to "14," got off, and another greeter in tails directed us to the elevator that would carry us to the top floor. Having arrived, the doors opened, and we were greeted this time by a lovely young lady dressed in white tails holding a silver tray with crystal flutes filled with delicious champagne. Flanking her, standing boldly against the wall, were two eight-foot "Oscar" statues. Incredible. Jerrene had left no stone unturned.

As we were guided into the room, I saw a myriad of Gary Clarke displays. Pictures and artifacts of virtually every phase of my life. One table even had tastefully arranged wedding photos of my three marriages. Jerrene and I moved around the room making sure we welcomed everyone. Speeches were made. I asked Dave to do his acceptance speech I'd written. He declined. Tony Butala, Jimmy Blaine, and I sang some of "our" songs. Then others got up and sang. Or did skits. Or told stories. Everyone participated.

Tables were unobtrusively set about the room, each one laden with memorabilia and souvenirs. Food tables were also strategically placed. One standout table was the one piled high with shrimp. Easily the most popular regarding food. Set right in the middle of the shrimp was a four-foot ice carving of a wild stallion reared up on its hind legs. Beautifully done and a marvel of balance. The chef came out and asked if everything was alright.

"Beyond my wildest dreams," said Jerrene.

"Who," I asked, " did that beautiful ice sculpture?"

The chef said that he had and was pleased that we liked it. About that time, Sheriff Joe came up and also spoke highly of the carving. I could tell that he was genuinely impressed. Then, with great deference, he touched the tail, ever so lightly, and it broke off. It fell right into the middle of all that shrimp. If Joe could have evaporated, he would have. And there was absolutely nothing to say except, "I am so sorry." He did and the chef made everything alright:

"It's okay, Sheriff Joe. That's what these carvings do when they start to melt." "I realize that," said Joe. "I just didn't want to be the one to help it along."

He apologized once again and walked off. For the rest of the night, whenever someone spoke, did a skit or even sang a song, they would find a way to mention Joe's "ripping the tail off a helpless stallion's butt."

Another extraordinary aspect of the evening was the 360-degree view of the city. Breathtaking. I don't know how Jerrene arranged it, but just as everyone was settling in, a thunderstorm presented itself and regaled us with an incomparable lightning display for the rest of the night.

Now, here's the really unbelievable part of this miraculous evening. It would appear that this extravaganza would have cost a fortune. Given the theater, the Bank One building, the limos, the hotel rooms for the out-of-towners, the tuxedos. And let's not forget all of the printing and duplicating and food and props and everything else I've forgotten to mention. Because of the people who jumped in to help Jerrene pull off this amazing event, and because all of them knew somebody who knew somebody, most everything was donated. Not all, but most. Things that people would do began to take on a life of their own. Somehow, the whole town began to buzz about "The Gary Clarke Film Festival." People felt the fun and wanted to play. Everybody knew. It seems the whole town knew. Except me. I knew nothing! Not an inkling. So much for "You can't surprise me!"

Most everything I've related to you over the last few pages, except when I was actually there, was all told to me later. That was twenty-three years ago, and I still love to hear Jerrene tell how it all unfolded. That night will be a night in my life that I will remember until the day I die, and even then I will take it with me. And, as I've said throughout this book, none of this would have ever happened were it not for every single person I've met, good, bad or indifferent, on my incredible journey through this business.

Natalie, Ava and a very blessed Dad.

Epilogue

I would be sadly remiss if I didn't place some of the credit for the writing of this book where that credit is due. The resurgence of popularity in *The Virginian* is due solely to those fans who were there when it first hit the air and to those who discovered us later. Their appreciation and willingness to tell us in no uncertain terms what the show meant and means to them can take your breath away. They have been the impetus for me to write, good or bad, about what it was like growing up in this phenomenal business. For me, it was like sitting on Babe all over again.

And personally, regarding my life outside the business, it has been joyous. Regardless of the road bumps, pitfalls, wrong turns, hiccups, and aches and pains, my Guardian Angels never let me down. Even during those times when my cockiness reared its ugly head and I'd say, "C'mon, guys. I can handle this on my own. Bug off. Take a siesta."

I've fallen on my butt, screwed up big time, done people dirty, or worse, and when I looked around, my Angels were still there. You may have guessed by now that I'm a believer and yes, Christ has played a important roll in my journey. My life is blessed and, given the opportunity, I wouldn't change a thing, except maybe . . . making a deal with God to keep my daughters from growing up so fast. Ava was born in 1993; Natalie was born in 2001. That makes Ava 22, going on 36, and Natalie 15, going on 35—she's gaining on Ava.

God bless you, your family, and our country.

Index